Bead Weaving
and Embroidery
with Miyuki Beads

STACKPOLE BOOKS

An imprint of Globe Pequot, the trade division of
The Rowman & Littlefield Publishing Group, Inc.
4501 Forbes Blvd., Ste. 200
Lanham, MD 20706
www.rowman.com
Distributed by NATIONAL BOOK NETWORK
800-462-6420

Copyright © 2020 Éditions Eyrolles, Paris, France
Original French title: *Tissage et broderie de perles miyuki*
Graphic design: Julie Simoens
Layout: STDI
Photographs: Sébastien Jarry
Charts: Virginie Châtenet
Cover: Studio Eyrolles / Sally Rinehart / photo Sébastien Jarry
The embroidery in the photos on pages 52 and 55 are from textile cards
made by the artisanal brand Cysé (https://cysenotebook.com).

We have made every effort to ensure the accuracy and completeness of
these instructions. We cannot, however, be responsible for human error,
typographical mistakes, or variations in individual work.

British Library Cataloguing in Publication Information available

Library of Congress Cataloging-in-Publication Data

Names: Châtenet, Virginie, author. | Châtenet, Virginie. Tissage et
  broderie de perles miyuki.
Title: Bead weaving and embroidery with miyuki beads / Virginie Châtenet.
Other titles: Tissage et broderie de perles miyuki. English
Description: First edition. | Guilford, Connecticut: Stackpole Books,
  [2021] | Summary: "Learn how to work brick stitch, peyote stitch, square
  stitch, and loom weaving. The stitches are explained in
  easy-to-understand steps and photos, with troubleshooting tips for
  success"— Provided by publisher.
Identifiers: LCCN 2021023211 (print) | LCCN 2021023212 (ebook) | ISBN
  9780811770095 (paperback) | ISBN 9780811770101 (epub)
Subjects: LCSH: Beadwork—Patterns. | Bead embroidery—Patterns.
Classification: LCC TT860 .C47513 2021 (print) | LCC TT860 (ebook) | DDC
  746.5—dc23
LC record available at https://lccn.loc.gov/2021023211
LC ebook record available at https://lccn.loc.gov/2021023212

First Edition

Bead Weaving and Embroidery with Miyuki Beads

Instructions for Brick Stitch, Peyote Stitch, Square Stitch, and Loom Work
100 WEAVING PATTERNS

Virginie Châtenet
from the blog *Des étoiles à la pistache*
Photographs by Sébastien Jarry

STACKPOLE
BOOKS

Guilford, Connecticut
Blue Ridge Summit, Pennsylvania

ACKNOWLEDGMENTS

As with my first book in French, *Brick Stitch: Méthode complète et motifs*, this second book would not have been possible without people in my life for whom I am extremely grateful. Among these, I would especially like to thank:

- **Aude, my editor:** Thank you, Aude, for your faith once again in this second book, your enthusiasm for my work, and your listening ear throughout the project. I couldn't wish for a better editor than you!

- **Maria, my editorial assistant:** Thank you, Maria, for your meticulous proofreading (and your eagle eye that misses nothing!) and the positive energy that you bring that just makes everything go well. It was a pleasure to find you for this second book.

- **The readers of my first book:** Thank you for trusting me, thank you for your enthusiastic feedback, for your very kind messages, and for sharing on social media. Thanks as well for having come to meet me at shows and bookstores during my book signings. I will never forget these opportunities to meet with you.

- **My Instagram and blog[1] followers:** Your likes, your comments, and the photos you have shared of projects completed thanks to my book are anything but virtual. They are a real and immense source of encouragement for me. Thanks for being there!

- **Céline, my yoga teacher (and all the yogis in my class):** Thank you, Céline, for those precious hours that make my Monday mornings brilliant, spreading their benefits to all days of the week and beyond. This book, like the previous one, would likely not be here if yoga had not come into my life.

- **My loved ones:** Friends and family, there are too many of you to mention individually, but you know who you are, because you know how much your

In my office-workshop, my own place where I have created, woven, and written much of this book.

bright presence means to me. When I think of each and every one of you while writing this, I see all the qualities you each possess and it is like a shower of little joys. Thanks for the extremely precious solid anchor you provide in my daily life.

And finally, a special thanks to:

- You, Sébastien Jarry, my life partner—your presence, your love, your human and artistic sensitivity, our mutual passion for nature (and our marvelous yard), our crazy projects in working toward a kinder and more respectful world, our hours of walking in nature, making my life so rich and beautiful! Thanks also for your talent and your total commitment in taking each photo for this book. This was a monumental task, and I'm so thankful that you put so much heart and professionalism into it.

- And you, Adrien and Timothée, my children born out of love. Every day I am so thankful that life has given me this happiness of being your mom. I love you, my little pirates!

---

1. *Des étoiles à la Pistache*, https://etoilespistache.wordpress.com/.

Acknowledgments

This book, as was my first, is dedicated to my mom, Christiane Staszewski-Châtenet, my absolute creative star.

I wish you could have seen this book, Mom. In these past ten years without you, each second spent creating is a moment that I'm with you again. This book is made up of thousands of moments with you. You are in each page.

I also dedicate this book to my father, Jacques Châtenet. You, my daddy, my sun, my beacon in the night. You who spread joy with unfailing generosity, you whose presence is always warm, you who taught me to love life no matter what. Thanks for being there, Dad.

•:•

A Few Words on My Vision of Creative Activities

My personal experience and the sharing of creative time with my friends or during workshops (as a participant or facilitator) make me think that having a creative outlet is a deeply stabilizing habit.

It's not just a way to "kill time," as we sometimes hear; rather, it's about nourishing your life. It's about taking time for yourself, living in the present (so you forget about past worries and future anxieties), and doing something soothing and rewarding.

The simple act of weaving a small pin or bracelet for oneself—or as a gift—results in much more than a piece of jewelry. Above all, by weaving, we give ourselves precious time to reconnect with ourselves. I often say that bead weaving, or any other creative or manual activity, is similar to meditation. No wonder so many people say how much they value that time.

By sharing my passion, I hope to sow small moments of peace and happiness. I also hope to weave connections and build bridges that will allow beautiful exchanges, beautiful encounters, beautiful times of sharing.

I worked on this book in this spirit: to offer you beautiful designs and especially some enjoyable times!

Wishing you a wonderful day and happy weaving!

CONTENTS

Part 3—Loom Weaving: Method and Patterns

Part 4—Square Stitch: Method and Patterns

Part 5—Bead Embroidery

Part 6—What to Do with Your Beadwork

INTRODUCTION

In this book, you will learn nine bead weaving techniques—the brick stitch; the even-count and odd-count peyote stitches; the circular, triangular, hexagonal, and pentagonal peyote stitches; loom weaving; and the square stitch—along with several bead embroidery stitches.

TECHNIQUES

Each of these techniques has its specific features, common points and differences, advantages and disadvantages.

In this book, the section on the Brick Stitch is extensive because the greatest variety of designs can be made with this stitch. You will find many patterns in here, grouped together by theme.

The Peyote Stitch, Square Stitch, and Loom Weaving sections offer various jewelry designs (bracelets, cuffs, pendants, necklaces, rings, etc.) that could also be used to personalize accessories.

Finally, a section of this book is dedicated to bead embroidery. Various stitches are explained that you can use to create beadwork and to complete projects that combine several techniques.

	Brick Stich	Peyote Stitch (in rows and rounds)	Loom Weaving	Square Stitch
Bead placement	In staggered rows.	In staggered rows.	Directly above and below each other using a loom.	Directly above and below each other.
Sequence of weaving	Bead by bead, straight rows worked back and forth.	**In rows:** bead by bead, in staggered rows and back and forth. **In rounds:** bead by bead or several beads together, in staggered rows and in rounds.	Row by row, all the beads of the row at the same time and back and forth.	Bead by bead, row in a straight line and back and forth.
Advantages	Can be used to weave all shapes. Easy-to-read charts (weaving in straight line).	**In rows:** quick and simple technique. **In rounds:** makes it possible to weave several geometric shapes (circle, triangle, hexagon, pentagon).	Quick and simple technique, especially suitable for weaving cuff-type bracelets.	May be used to obtain the same finished product as with loom weaving but without a loom.
Disadvantages	Long weaving. For complex designs, it is necessary to know how to do several stitches.	Charts difficult to read (weaving in staggered rows). Techniques limited to simple shapes.	Technique limited to simple shapes. Requires a loom.	Technique that only works with small designs and simple shapes.
Weaving speed	Slow: bead by bead, thread passes through each bead several times.	Quick: bead by bead (or several beads together). Thread passes through a single time.	Very quick: row by row.	Slow: bead by bead, thread passes through each bead several times.

MATERIALS

You will need the following materials to complete your beadwork:

- A needle (extra fine with a narrow eye). I prefer Tulip size 10 needles or Miyuki beading needles. For loom weaving, make sure the needle is at least 2 in. (5.1 cm) long (or even longer depending on the width of the bracelet).

- Fine nylon thread (0.20 mm). I use SoNo beading thread, One-G beading thread, or Miyuki Beading Thread size B for peyote stitch and loom weaving. I prefer to use FireLine thread (0.10 mm) for the brick stitch and the square stitch; it is finer and stiffer in addition to being as strong as the previous ones. Test them and use the thread that works best for you.

- And beads, of course! Cylindrical glass seed beads are used that stack perfectly one on the other, making for very smooth and even weaving. Use Miyuki Delica beads size 11/0 (the most well known) or 1.8 mm Toho Treasures, less well known but also good quality. For some of the beadwork, Miyuki Bugle beads, size 3 mm or 6 mm, are also used. These are small, tube-shaped beads. In each pattern where beads are mentioned, "DB" is used for Delica beads and "BGL" is used for Bugle beads.

- **For loom weaving:** a loom. Whatever brand, material, or price, make sure that the size is large enough for a bracelet at least 5 in. (13 cm) long.

> TIP
>
> **Avoid Round Beads**
>
> Seed beads or rocailles are often round and not cylindrical. If you use them in your projects:
>
> - the weaving will be more difficult,
> - the end product will be much more uneven (and therefore not as pretty), and
> - it will be more difficult to attach fasteners to the beadwork.
>
> If you have a stash of them, they would be better used in embroidery.

To turn your beadwork into jewelry or decorative items, you will need some additional items, depending on your project and your tastes.

- Pin backs (size depends on your beadwork)
- Jewelry and bead glue to attach the beadwork to the pin back
- Earring hooks or earring bases
- Chains (if you want to make a necklace or bracelet)
- Clasps for necklaces or bracelets
- Jump rings to connect beadwork to a chain and the chain to a clasp
- Specific end bars or backings to professionally finish off woven bead bracelets
- Other items as desired

NOTE

In the section "What to Do with Your Beadwork" (page 166), you will find several ideas and tutorials that include detailed lists of the materials needed for the projects.

HOW TO STIFFEN YOUR BEADWORK

Beadwork is relatively supple, which can be inconvenient for some uses, particularly when you wish to transform a design larger than 1.2 in. (3 cm) into a pin.

To make beadwork stiffer, simply apply a thin coat of Décopatch varnish (hypoallergenic or not, depending on use) to the back of your work.

Let dry completely before assembling your beadwork into a piece of jewelry.

MY MAIN ADVICE

The most important advice is to stitch with a light hand, pulling on the thread gently to avoid knots. Take your time. Bead weaving is a type of needlework, and like all needlework, it requires patience and precision.

Patience is especially needed at the start, when you stitch the first rows, because there is not much to hold on to and the beads can move if they are not held firmly. Once this step is over, the beads will not move, and it will be much easier to handle the beadwork and get the hang of the technique.

When choosing a brick stitch pattern, if you are a beginner, it will be better to start with a simple pattern (level 1 or 2). The little stars indicate level of difficulty.

Do what makes you happy; change colors to create variations and adapt the patterns to your own taste.

When selecting your colors, choose shades by arranging a few beads of each color on a small tray and see whether the color of any beads is quite different compared to the others. Indeed, the color of the beads in the middle of a bag (which contains more than 1,000 beads) will always be more intense; therefore, it's better to take out some of them to get an idea of the final version and not be disappointed in the middle of a project.

PART 1

BRICK STITCH: METHODS AND PATTERNS

The first part of this section offers all the technical instructions needed to help you learn how to weave the brick stitch.

The second part offers several beadwork patterns with charts, along with some variations.

To find ideas that will bring your beadwork to life (jewelry, accessories, decorative items, etc.), go to the end of the book in the section "What to Do with Your Beadwork" (page 166).

BEFORE STARTING

A bit of advice for beginners: Read this section thoroughly before starting. Here you will find all the basic advice needed for your first experience to be a success. ;-)

READING A BEAD WEAVING CHART

General Information

Brick stitch is stitched in a straight line, row by row, in one direction and then the other: from left to right, then right to left, or from bottom to top, then top to bottom. Whatever direction is shown in the chart, this is the direction the beads are to be stitched.

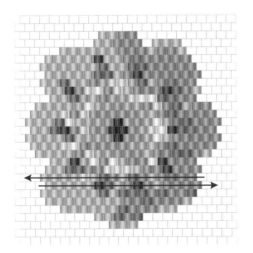

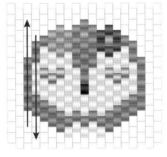

Work the first row from bottom to top, the next from top to bottom, and so on.

Each new row of beads is offset from the previous row (like the construction of a brick wall).

Work the first row from left to right, the next from right to left, and so on.

The First Steps

Stitching begins at the point indicated by the arrow, regardless of the method selected.

There are two methods that can be used to start the brick stitch: start with one row (ladder stitch) or start with two rows. The two starting rows are shown in the red frame in the chart. Start on the side indicated by the arrow.

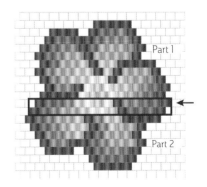

Part 1

Part 2

For a one-row start, the arrow indicates the first row and the side from which you should start.

Starting a Project

Next to the starting row(s) of the beadwork are the indications "Part 1" and "Part 2." They show where part 1 of the design begins, followed by part 2. Start by stitching your first row or two rows, and then continue with part 1. When that is finished, weave in your thread and cut it. Then pick up the second thread and start part 2. If the design has two parts, the pattern is finished when you reach the end of this second part. For more complex designs, the remaining parts must be completed as indicated on the chart.

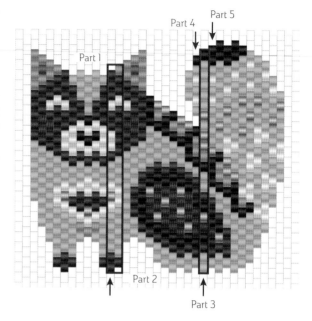

For some complex designs like this one, the charts will be marked in several places to indicate the sequence in which the different parts are to be worked.

You will find the Large Cats on page 68.

- 14 -

STITCHES

Here you will find the brick stitch weaving technique explained step by step.

STARTING A PROJECT

Method 1: The "Classic" Ladder Stitch Start

With this technique, the first row is completed using the ladder stitch. It is the only row that will be made this way. This method is the one used most often, which is why I call it "classic."

The principle is very simple, but it requires some dexterity to keep the beads from twisting around. I would advise beginners to use FireLine thread (between 0.10 mm and 0.18 mm), hold the beads woven together tightly between two fingers, and add each bead carefully, pulling on the thread slowly.

For this first example, we will follow the chart below.

Starting row. The arrow indicates the first bead.

Prepare your thread (about 3 ft./1 m) and your needle. Don't knot the end of the thread.

Pick up the first two beads in your pattern with your needle. Here, the first bead is red and the second is blue.

Place the beads in the middle of the thread so that there are about 20 in. (50 cm) of thread on each side of the bead.

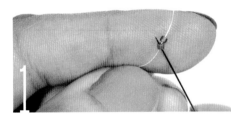

Hold the thread and the beads on top of your index finger to keep them in place.

Pass the needle through the first bead of the row, the one on the bottom (the red bead).

STEP 1

In the above photo, I place the thread over my finger so that the first bead—the red one—is on the bottom. The working thread connected to the needle is coming out the top of the bead, going behind the finger, forming a loop. The "free" end of the thread is going down from the finger and is held in place by the thumb.

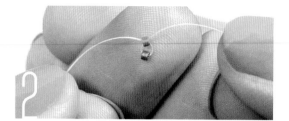

Pull gently on your thread until tightened, and the beads will line up like a ladder, one above the other.

TIP

Reinforce the Starting Ladder Stitch

When you're just starting out, I would advise you to stitch through the first two beads a second time to make sure they're firmly in place and keep them from twisting later. To do this, pass through the blue bead again, and then through the red one, repeating the first thread path.

Important: Starting with this step, go slowly and carefully, holding your beads firmly between your thumb and fingers.

The first row is a bit tricky; these beads have a tendency to twist if they are not held firmly. If that happens to you, don't panic! Simply reposition the beads carefully in the right direction and hold them in place again.

Before adding the third bead, the thread must be brought back through the blue bead.

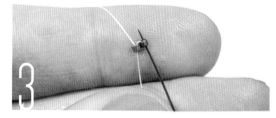

Bring the needle through the blue bead and pull the thread all the way through.

The two threads should be parallel in the two beads. Hold the threads firmly in this orientation so that the beads don't change position.

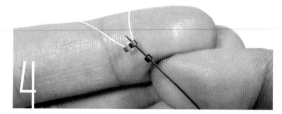

Pick up the third bead of your pattern (in this case, a gray bead) with the needle. Then pass the needle through the blue bead already in place (the thread is coming out the top, the needle enters through the bottom).

Before picking up the fourth bead of your pattern, you need to position the thread in the last bead added (here, the gray bead).

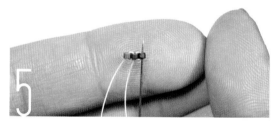

Pass the needle through the gray bead and gently pull the thread all the way through.

Always be thinking about holding your beads firmly and keeping the threads in the direction they exit the beads (especially do not pull the threads in the direction of the row of beads). The beads must be in the form of a ladder (openings one on top of the other) rather than in a line (openings facing each other).

Continue in this manner until your first row is finished:

- pick up a new bead,
- pass needle through the last bead added to the end of the row,
- pull thread to position the new bead,
- pass needle through the bead just added so that the thread is exiting at the end of the row; repeat steps.

When your first row is completed, you can begin a new row (see page 19).

Method 2: Bead the First Two Rows at Once

To my knowledge, in France, where I'm from, there is no tutorial on this method. I found out about it thanks to a Canadian beader, who learned of it from an American beader. After testing it, I was completely convinced this technique is much easier to use than the first one, even if it seems more complex at first.

This method will be better for beginners in particular (who might not be used to using the needle and thread); there is almost no risk of the beads twisting. This is the method I now use to start all of my beadwork.

In this book, these two rows are outlined on each chart.

For this example, we will look at the following chart.

The arrows indicate the two starting rows and the first three beads, which are, in order, red, blue, and gray.

Prepare your thread (about 3 ft./1 m) and your needle. Don't knot the end of the thread.

Pick up the first three beads in the chart with your needle. For this example,

- the first bead is red,

- the second is blue,

- the third is gray.

Place the beads in the middle of the thread.

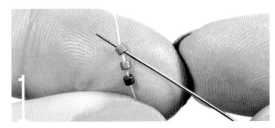

Pick up the first three beads (red, blue, gray). Hold the thread and the beads on your finger to keep them in place.

Pass the needle through the first bead (the top one, the red bead).

STEP 1

In the above photo, I place the thread over my finger so that the first bead—the red one—is on top. The thread leaving the needle and going toward the gray bead is therefore on the bottom and the tail of the thread is on the top.

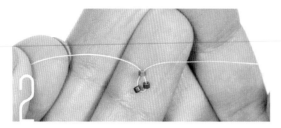

By gently pulling your thread all the way through, the beads will move into position to form a small triangle. The two ends of the thread are now coming out of the first bead.

Pick up the fourth bead of your pattern (here a pink bead).

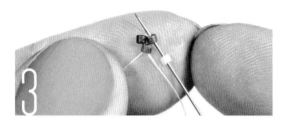

After picking up the fourth bead in your chart (the pink bead) with the needle, pass the needle through the blue bead already in place in the top row. The needle enters through the bottom of the bead and comes out the top.

Pick up the fifth bead of your pattern, here the green bead.

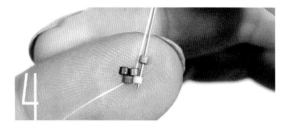

Pass the needle through the light pink bead. The needle enters from the top of the bead and the thread comes out the bottom.

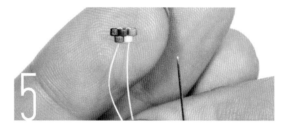

The fifth bead in the chart (the green one) is now in place.

Continue in this manner until your first double row is completed.

When your first two rows are done, you can begin a new row.

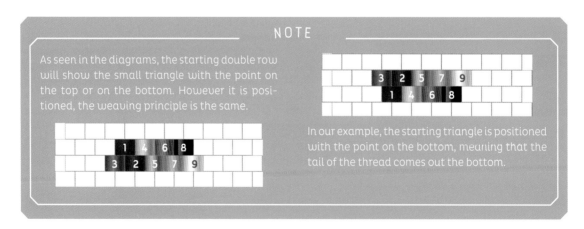

NOTE

As seen in the diagrams, the starting double row will show the small triangle with the point on the top or on the bottom. However it is positioned, the weaving principle is the same.

In our example, the starting triangle is positioned with the point on the bottom, meaning that the tail of the thread comes out the bottom.

STARTING A NEW ROW

Different scenarios may arise when starting a new row: a single or multiple increase, a single or multiple decrease (even or odd number for the latter). You must check the chart to see which one it is.

In the instructions below, the new row starts on the right and goes to the left. The principle is exactly the same if the new row starts on the left and goes to the right.

Starting a New Row with a Single Increase

For a single increase, the first bead in the new row overhangs the previous row.

For this example, we will follow the diagram below.

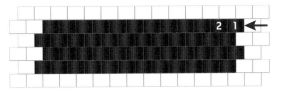

The new row to be stitched at the top begins with a single increase on the right with a blue bead and then a red bead.

Pick up the first two beads in your chart with your needle (in this case, a blue bead and then a red bead).

Pass your needle under the thread bridge, the exposed thread connecting the last two beads of the row below.

Gently pull the thread all the way through. The two beads will fall into position to form the new overhanging row.

Pass your needle through the bottom and out the top of the red bead.

You will now be able to continue your row, adding one bead at a time (see "Continuing a Row One Bead at a Time," page 24).

Starting a New Row with a Multiple Increase

For a multiple increase, the new row overhangs the previous row by two or more beads. This will be found especially on the more complicated patterns. It is better to avoid tackling this type of pattern at the very beginning and to wait until you have mastered the technique to try this stitch.

For this example, we will follow the diagram below.

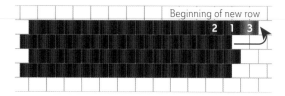

The new row to be added (at the top) begins with a multiple increase on the right.

Start with a single increase using the method described above, with beads 1 and 2 (the blue and the red). Then continue with the ladder stitch method (see "Method 1: The 'Classic' Ladder Stitch Start" in the section "Starting a Project").

Pass your needle from top to bottom through the end bead (the blue one).

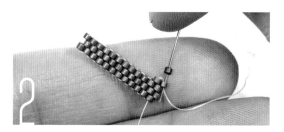

Pick up the second increase bead according to your pattern (here the gray bead) and again pass through the blue bead from top to bottom.

The second increase bead is in place.

If your pattern requires more increases, continue in the same manner (that is, using the ladder stitch). To do this, pass your needle through the bead that you just placed (here the gray bead that is on the edge). Pick up the next bead, and then pass the needle from bottom to top through the last bead set in place (the gray bead). Continue in this manner for the next beads, if required by the pattern.

When you have increased the number of beads as shown in your pattern, you must return to where you started the row to continue working the pattern.

To do this, pass your needle through each bead until you reach the spot where you started the row.

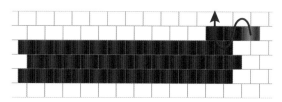

Pass your needle from one bead to the next (from top to bottom and then bottom to top) to return to the starting bead.

To continue the row, your thread must come out the top of the bead on the end.

Depending on the increased number of beads, the thread may or may not come out of the end bead in the proper direction. If it does not come out in the right direction, follow the thread path shown in the diagram on the next page.

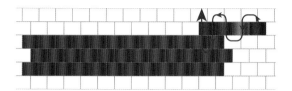

Your thread is now in the proper position, and you can continue your row bead by bead (see "Continuing a Row One Bead at a Time," page 24).

Starting a New Row with a Single Decrease

For a single decrease, the new row will have one fewer bead than the previous row.

In this example, we will follow the diagram below.

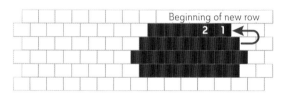

The new row to be added (on top) starts with a single decrease on the right with a red bead and then a blue bead.

With your needle, pick up the first two beads in your chart (in this case, the red bead and then the blue bead).

Bring your needle under the thread bridge between the second and third bead of the previous row.

Pull on the thread gently all the way to the end. The two beads will move into place to begin to form a new decrease row (at this stage, the beads will not yet be perfectly in place, but that's normal).

TIP

Invisible Decreases

With this method, no threads will show on the sides of the bead. I actually see a lot of tutorials and patterns on Instagram with decreases where the thread is visible. I also started like that, but, not finding it very attractive, I looked for and found a solution on the internet, which I am sharing with you here because it allows you to achieve a beautiful result.

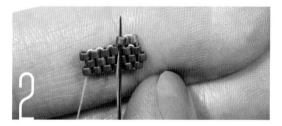

Pass your needle through the blue bead from bottom to top.

Then pass through the red bead from top to bottom.

Starting with this next step, there are two methods available, and you can choose either one.

Method 1 is quicker and simpler than method 2, but the advantage of the latter is that it locks the beads in place more securely, which can be useful for some designs. However, you are free to use whichever one you prefer.

Method 1

Pass the needle through the blue bead from bottom to top.

Methods 1 and 2 (continued)

Method 2

Pass your needle through the second bead of the previous row, from top to bottom.

Pass the needle through the third bead of the previous row, from bottom to top, and then through the second bead of the new row.

Pull gently on the thread to move the beads into their proper position.

Now you can continue your row bead by bead (see "Continuing a Row One Bead at a Time," page 24).

Starting a New Row with a Multiple Decrease

For a multiple decrease, the new row will have two or more fewer beads than the previous row.

"Multiple decrease" is a bit of a misnomer, as it simply involves placing the thread in the right location, with either a single increase or a single decrease, in the row just added in order to start a new row.

Example 1: Decrease of 2, 4, 6 (or Any Other Even Number) Beads from the Edge

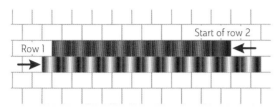

The new row starts here on the right with the decrease of two beads from the edge.

Before picking up the first two beads of your new row, first follow the path shown by the arrow below to reposition your thread in the right location.

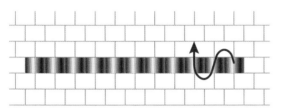

Going from top to bottom, without picking up a new bead, pass through the second gray bead from the edge and then from bottom to top through the next bead.

NOTE

Repeat this step once if you are decreasing four beads from the edge and twice if six beads, and so forth.

Your thread is now coming out the top of the bead indicated by the red arrow. You can start your new row using the single increase technique when starting a row.

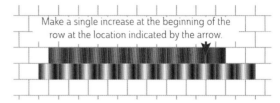

Start your new row where the thread exits, here with a blue bead and a red bead, making a single increase at the beginning of the row (page 19).

Continue your row, adding one bead at a time (see "Continuing a Row One Bead at a Time," page 24).

Example 2: Decrease of 3, 5, 7 (or Any Other Odd Number) Beads from the Edge

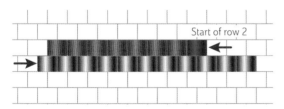

The new row starts here on the right with the decrease of three beads from the edge.

Before picking up the first two beads of your new row, first follow the path shown by the arrow in the diagram on the right to reposition your thread in the right location.

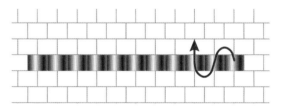

Pass from top to bottom, without picking up a new bead, through the second gray bead from the edge, and then from bottom to top through the next bead.

NOTE

Repeat this step once if you are decreasing five beads from the edge, twice if seven beads, and so on.

Your thread is now coming out the top of the bead indicated by the red arrow. You can start your new row using the single decrease technique when starting a row.

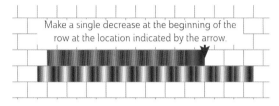

Start your new row where the thread comes up, here with a blue bead and a red bead, making a single decrease at the beginning of the row (page 21).

Continue your row, adding one bead at a time (see "Continuing a Row One Bead at a Time," below).

CONTINUING A ROW ONE BEAD AT A TIME

Once your new row is started with an increase (single or multiple) or a decrease (single or multiple), you will be able to continue it by now going bead by bead.

With your needle, pick up the bead shown on your pattern (in this case, the gray bead).

Pass your needle under the thread bridge connecting the two beads from the row below.

Pull gently on your thread all the way to the end. Your bead will position itself on the row.

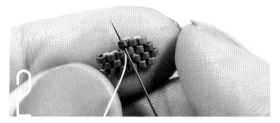

Now pass from bottom to top through the bead that you just added.

Continue in this manner, following your pattern.

If your row ends with an increase (single or multiple), read the instructions below ("Ending a Row with an Increase") to continue. If not, start your new row.

ENDING A ROW WITH AN INCREASE

Different scenarios may come up regarding how you need to finish a row.

Ending a Row with a Single Increase

When your pattern requires that your row must end with an increase compared to the previous row, here is what to do.

In this example, we will follow the diagram below.

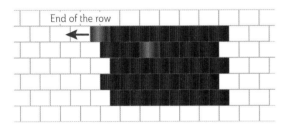

End of the row

The top row here ends on the left with a single increase (gray bead).

Pick up the gray bead you will use for the increase.

Pass between the last bead of the row (blue one) and the last bead of the row below (the red one).

Gently pull on the thread all the way to the end and position the bead at the end of the row (help it if needed; it may not fall into place by itself).

Then pass from bottom to top through the bead that you just added (the gray one).

Pull gently on the thread until the bead is correctly in place.

Ending a Row with a Multiple Increase

When your pattern requires that your row must end with an increase of several beads compared to the previous row, here is what to do.

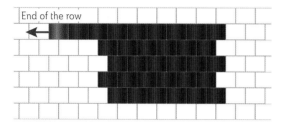

Here the row ends with a multiple increase: red, blue, and gray beads.

End your row by making a single increase at the end of the row, here with the red bead.

Continue your row with the ladder stitch (see "Method 1: The 'Classic' Ladder Stitch Start," page 15). To do this, pick up your bead (here, a blue bead) and pass your needle from bottom to top through the last bead in the row (the red one).

Pull gently on the thread, and your bead will fall into place at the end of the row.

If you need to add another bead (here, the gray one), pass from top to bottom through the bead that you just set in place (the blue one). Then pick up the next bead (the gray one) and pass from bottom to top through the last bead of the row (the blue one).

Continue in this manner for each increase indicated by your chart.

STITCHING ON AN ISOLATED BEAD

Two methods are available, each with a different look.

Method 1

Stitch on the bead like any other bead in a normal row. Pick up your bead and pass your needle under the thread bridge between the two beads from the row below. Then pass through the bead that you just added.

With this technique, the thread is visible on the side of the bead. It's a bit unsightly, but it's the only way to add an isolated bead and have it face the right direction.

Method 2

With this method, the thread is not visible on the side, but the bead is positioned in the opposite direction from the others.

To do this, pick up the bead and pass from top to bottom through the bead located next to the one the thread is exiting.

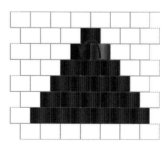

In method 2, the thread comes out of the gray bead. After picking up the blue bead, pass from top to bottom through the red bead. The blue bead will fall into place in the opposite direction from the others, which is not the case in the diagram.

REPOSITIONING THE THREAD

The principle of the brick stitch is to add beads row after row following a chart. When the design includes rows with a break in them (as in Diagram 1, circled in red), or the gap is too large between two consecutive rows, it is necessary to interrupt the stitching and resume at a different position.

The principle consists of determining the bead where the thread must exit and then passing the thread through the beadwork to that spot, in order to continue the pattern at the right location.

In Diagram 2, the stitching ends where the arrow starts and must then continue with the bead circled in green.

The path shown by the arrow is where the thread must go so it can come up through the bead at the end.

This way, the thread will be at the right spot to restart the stitching at the bead circled in green.

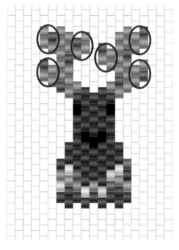

Diagram 1

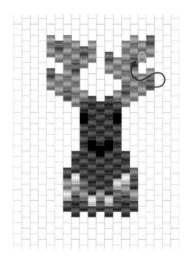

Diagram 2

FINISHING A PROJECT

Once your last bead has been stitched on, you will need to weave the thread through several beads in the piece to secure it before cutting (the thread is never knotted).

The idea is to pass the thread through the beadwork in order to form a little loop that will secure the thread. Then cut the thread as close to the beadwork as possible, so that the end does not stick out, preferably using small embroidery scissors or small cutting pliers (jewelry tools) to do this.

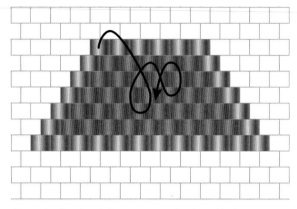

Example of path to follow to secure the thread before cutting.

CHANGING THREAD

If you see that your thread is going to be too short to finish your project, change it when it is still at least 6 in. (15 cm) long.

First secure your thread as if you were finishing a project (see above). Then attach a new thread to be able to continue stitching.

To do this, the principle is the same as for securing the end of the thread. You need to form a little loop that will secure the thread and then position it in the right spot to continue your beadwork where you left off.

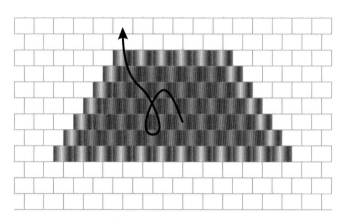

Example of how to add and secure a new thread.

BRICK STITCH PATTERNS

Each of the 80 patterns will include the following information:

- The pattern's level of difficulty on a scale of 1 to 4.
  - **Level 1** (beginner) is not difficult and is ideal for beginners and for learning basic techniques.
  - **Level 2** (beginner) is also suitable for beginners and allows you to try some slightly more difficult techniques, such as multiple decreases at the beginning of a row and repositioning the thread.
  - **Level 3** (intermediate) requires that you be comfortable with the basic techniques. This level adds in more difficult stitches, such as multiple increases at the end of a row and especially at the beginning of a row.
  - **Level 4** (expert) is for experts and those who want to try more complex (and/or longer) designs. These designs require patience, concentration, and careful precision, but you will be proud to complete them and will then no longer be afraid to tackle any bead weaving design.
- The size of the finished beadwork.
- The stitches used in the pattern.
- Color references for the Miyuki Delica 11/0 or Toho Treasure beads used.

- **Charts** that show:
  - where to begin stitching (the arrow indicates the side on which to start the first row or rows, depending on the method used);
  - the sequence of where to go next once you have completed the starting row or rows (for the different parts of the beadwork); and
  - the bead color references (to help you avoid the wrong color when adding beads).

Each pattern will also contain pictures and sometimes offer variations. You will discover many ideas and detailed tutorials in the "What to Do with Your Beadwork" section on page 166.

For each theme, you will also find a quote related to the section's patterns and ideas. This is a way for me to share my literary, poetic, or philosophical favorites with you.

IN THE FOREST

And they give off an odor, not of a dead room, not of sacristies and
cobwebs, but an odor of a vegetal space, of sudden gusts of wind swooping
down in wild swirls of feathers, leaves, and pollen from the infinite forest.

—Pablo Neruda, *The Luminous Solitude*

I like to walk in the forest, especially when there aren't too many others there. The ideal is actually to go on horseback, in silence, to have a better chance of seeing animals that live there and to enjoy a concert of bird songs.

There are always a thousand little treasures to be found in the forest—leaves, feathers, pieces of bark, stones, and so on—and you can also feel a tremendous energy, this breathing that we share with the trees. In the same way as for oceans, the protection and preservation of forests are, in my opinion, absolutely essential.

BRING YOUR BEADWORK TO LIFE

All of the projects in this section can be worn as a pin or be framed. You can also use them to make necklaces (with the owl heads or the "Flower" Leaves), longer necklaces (with the Autumn Birds), or earrings (with the Raindrops). To transform your beadwork projects into accessories, go to page 166.

TWIN LEAVES ★★★☆

Difficult stitches used:
- multiple decrease at beginning of row (see page 22)
- multiple increase at end of row (see page 26)

GREEN LEAVES

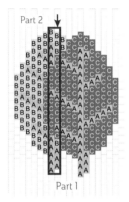

Part 2

Part 1

Color Key

DB-1152   DB-1814

DB-0829

A: DB-1152 (Matte Gold)
B: DB-0829 (Pale Moss)
C: DB-1814 (Emerald)

Size: 1¼ × 1 in. (3.3 × 2.4 cm)

PINK AND YELLOW LEAVES

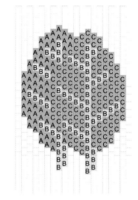

Color Key

DB-2114   DB-1152

DB-2102

A: DB-2114 (Light Watermelon)
B: DB-1152 (Matte Gold)
C: DB-2102 (Banana)

Size: 1¼ × 1 in. (3.3 × 2.4 cm)

1 Choose your starting method and follow the sequence of stitching as indicated on the chart.

2 To complete any difficult stitch, go to the page explaining that stitch.

3 When your beadwork is completed, secure and cut your thread; see instructions on page 28.

4 There are several ways you can finish up your project. Find all our ideas in part 6, beginning on page 166.

BIRD OF PARADISE ★★★☆

Difficult stitches used:
- multiple decrease at beginning of row (see page 22)
- multiple increase at end of row (see page 26)
- isolated bead (see page 26)

1　Choose your starting method and follow the sequence of stitching as indicated on the chart. To simplify things, I indicate the point where it is easiest to start and thereby avoid multiple increases at the beginning of a row, which is even more difficult than multiple increases at the end of a row.

2　To complete any difficult stitch, go to the page explaining that stitch.

3　When your beadwork is completed, secure and cut your thread; see instructions on page 28.

4　There are several ways you can finish up your project. Find all our ideas in part 6, beginning on page 166.

Color Key

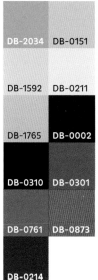

DB-2034	DB-0151
DB-1592	DB-0211
DB-1765	DB-0002
DB-0310	DB-0301
DB-0761	DB-0873
DB-0214	

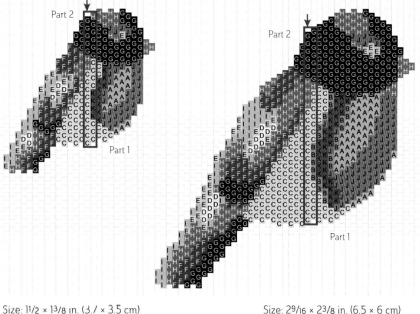

Size: 1¹/₂ × 1³/₈ in. (3.7 × 3.5 cm)

Size: 2⁹/₁₆ × 2³/₈ in. (6.5 × 6 cm)

A: DB-2034 (Luminous Flamingo)
B: DB-0151 (Orange)
C: DB-1592 (Canary)
D: DB-0211 (Limestone)
E: DB-1765 (Celery)
F: DB-0002 (Metallic Dark Blue)
G: DB-0310 (Matte Black)
H: DB-0301 (Matte Gunmetal)
I: DB-0761 (Gray)
J: DB-0873 (Vermilion)
K: DB-0214 (Red Luster)

AUTUMN BIRDS ★★★☆

Difficult stitches used:
- multiple decrease at beginning of row (see page 22)
- isolated bead (see page 26)
- repositioning the thread (see page 27)

The two bird designs are fairly easy to complete for the most part. The main difficulty comes at the beak and the end of the tail feathers, as the thread must be repositioned several times.

1   Choose your starting method and follow the sequence of stitching as indicated on the chart.

2   To complete any difficult stitch, go to the page explaining that stitch.

3   When your beadwork is completed, secure and cut your thread; see instructions on page 28.

4   There are several ways you can finish up your project. Find all our ideas in part 6, beginning on page 166.

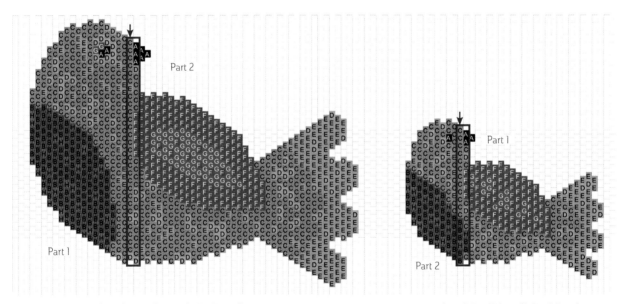

Size: 2³/₁₆ × 2⁷/₈ in. (5.5 × 7.4 cm)   Size: 1¹/₄ × 1³/₄ in. (3.3 × 4.5 cm)

Color Key

DB-0010	DB-0795	DB-2287	DB-2107	DB-2106	DB-0306	DB-2316

A: DB-0010 (Black)
B: DB-0795 (Cinnabar)
C: DB-2287 (Persimmon)
D: DB-2107 (Cedar)

E: DB-2106 (Hawthorne)
F: DB-0306 (Charcoal)
G: DB-2316 (Moody Blue)
H: DB-2275 (Glazed Opaque Red)

"FLOWER" LEAVES ★★★☆

Difficult stitches used:
- multiple decrease at beginning of row (see page 22)
- repositioning the thread (see page 27)

For the general steps, see opposite page.

FALL LEAVES

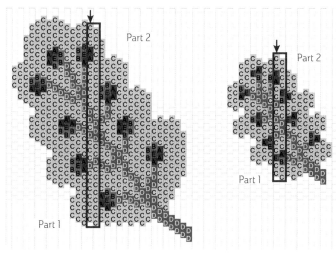

Size: 2 × 19/16 in. (5 × 4 cm)

Size: 11/8 × 1 in. (2.9 × 2.4 cm)

Color Key

DB-2173	DB-2275	DB-2290
DB-2312	DB-2306	

A: DB-2173 (Semi-Frosted Watermelon)
B: DB-2275 (Glazed Opaque Red)
C: DB-2290 (Honeydew)
D: DB-2312 (Thyme)
E: DB-2306 (Matte Brick)

SPRING LEAVES

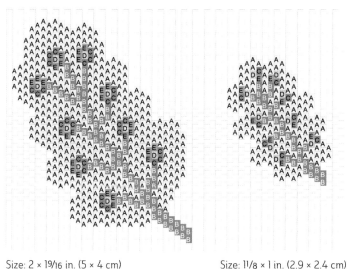

Size: 2 × 19/16 in. (5 × 4 cm)

Size: 11/8 × 1 in. (2.9 × 2.4 cm)

Color Key

DB-1516	DB-2311	DB-2118
DB-1906	DB-1742	

A: DB-1516 (Light Mint Green)
B: DB-2311 (Matte Dark Seafoam)
C: DB-2118 (Pansy)
D: DB-1906 (Rosewater)
E: DB-1742 (Rose)

OWLS ★★☆☆

Difficult stitch used: multiple decrease at beginning of row (see page 22)

1 Choose your starting method and follow the sequence of stitching as indicated on the chart.

2 To complete any difficult stitch, go to the page explaining that stitch.

3 When your beadwork is completed, secure and cut your thread; see instructions on page 28.

4 There are several ways you can finish up your project. Find all our ideas in part 6, beginning on page 166.

OWLS WITH BLUE FLOWERS

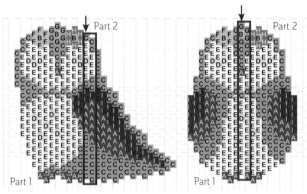

Size: 1³/8 × 1¹/2 in. (3.5 × 3.8 cm)

Size: 1³/8 × 1 in. (3.5 × 2.5 cm)

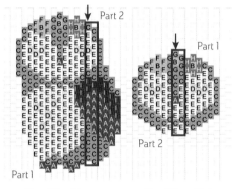

Size: 1³/8 × 1 in. (3.5 × 2.4 cm)

Size: 11/16 × 3/4 in. (1.8 × 2 cm)

Color Key

DB-2288	DB-0208	DB-2107
DB-0411	DB-0352	
DB-2129	DB-0267	
DB-2144	DB-2119	

A: DB-2288 (Sienna)
B: DB-0208 (Tan Luster)
C: DB-2107 (Cedar)
D: DB-0411 (Gold)
E: DB-0352 (Cream)
F: DB-2129 (Moody Blue)
G: DB-0267 (Blueberry Luster)
H: DB-2144 (Matte French Navy)
I: DB-2119 (Red Date)

OWLS WITH MULTICOLOR FLOWERS

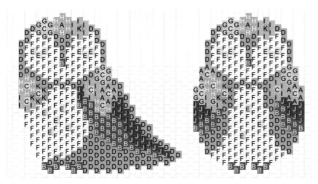

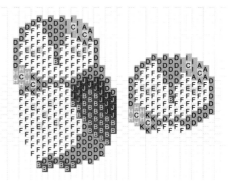

Size: 1³/₈ × 1¹/₂ in. (3.5 × 3.8 cm)

Size: 1³/₈ × 1 in. (3.5 × 2.5 cm)

Size: 1³/₈ × 1 in. (3.5 × 2.4 cm)

Size: 11/16 × 3/4 in. (1.8 × 2 cm)

Color Key

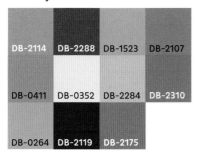

DB-2114 / DB-2288 / DB-1523 / DB-2107
DB-0411 / DB-0352 / DB-2284 / DB-2310
DB-0264 / DB-2119 / DB-2175

A: DB-2114 (Light Watermelon)
B: DB-2288 (Sienna)
C: DB-1523 (Light Salmon)
D: DB-2107 (Cedar)
E: DB-0411 (Gold)
F: DB-0352 (Cream)
G: DB-2284 (Pineapple)
H: DB-2310 (Pistachio)
I: DB-0264 (Mallard Luster)
J: DB-2119 (Red Date)
K: DB-2175 (Hibiscus)

OWLS WITHOUT FLOWERS

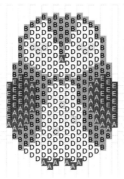

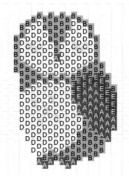

Size: 1³/₈ × 1¹/₂ in. (3.5 × 3.8 cm)

Size: 1³/₈ × 1 in. (3.5 × 2.5 cm)

Size: 1³/₈ × 1 in. (3.5 × 2.4 cm)

Color Key

DB-2288 / DB-2107 / DB-0411 / DB-0352 / DB-2119

A: DB-2288 (Sienna)
B: DB-2107 (Cedar)
C: DB-0411 (Gold)
D: DB-0352 (Cream)
E: DB-2119 (Red Date)

OAK LEAF ★★☆☆

Difficult stitch used: multiple decrease at beginning of row (see page 22)

This small and simple leaf is ideal for making a small pin.

1. Choose your starting method and follow the sequence of stitching as indicated on the chart.

2. To complete any difficult stitch, go to the page explaining that stitch.

3. When your beadwork is completed, secure and cut your thread; see instructions on page 28.

4. There are several ways you can finish up your project. Find all our ideas in part 6, beginning on page 166.

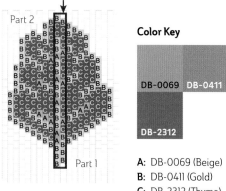

Size: 1³⁄₈ × 1 in. (3.5 × 2.4 cm)

Color Key

DB-0069   DB-0411

DB-2312

A: DB-0069 (Beige)
B: DB-0411 (Gold)
C: DB-2312 (Thyme)

FEATHER ★★☆☆

Difficult stitch used: multiple decrease at beginning of row (see page 22)

This pattern became a part of the book following a conversation with Nathalie, who loves and knows a lot about birds and who helped me identify feathers I had found in the forest. So thank you again, Nathalie. This pattern is specially dedicated to you!

1 Choose your starting method and follow the sequence of stitching as indicated on the chart. If you start with two rows, you will need to weave in a bead at the end of the row by positioning your thread at the end of the longest row and then stitching on an additional bead (see instructions for the multiple increase at end of row on page 26).

2 To complete any difficult stitch, go to the page explaining that stitch.

3 When your beadwork is completed, secure and cut your thread; see instructions on page 28.

4 There are several ways you can finish up your project. Find all our ideas in part 6, beginning on page 166.

Part 1

Part 2

Size: 2³/4 × ¹¹/16 in. (6.9 × 1.7 cm)

Color Key

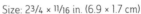

DB-0040	DB-1016
DB-0378	DB-2274
DB-0734	DB-0191

A: DB-0040 (Copper)
B: DB-1016 (Metallic Rhubarb)
C: DB-0378 (Matte Brick Red)
D: DB-2274 (Glazed Persimmon)
E: DB-0734 (Chocolate)
F: DB-0191 (Light Copper)

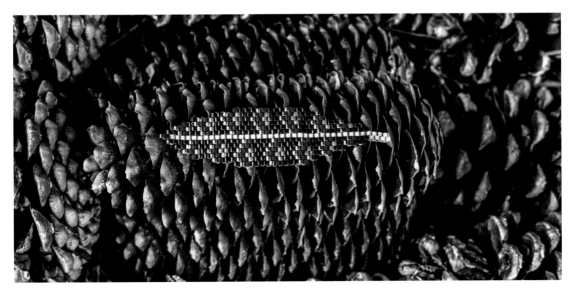

RAINDROPS ★★☆☆

Difficult stitch used: multiple decrease at beginning of row (see page 22)

The eight raindrop patterns are all very simple to make and are therefore perfect for starting out. However, be sure to carefully follow the charts; most of the designs are not symmetrical.

1 Choose your starting method and follow the sequence of stitching as indicated on the chart. For Raindrops 7 and 8, I would suggest you start with one row (ladder stitch). For the others, use your preferred method.

2 To complete any difficult stitch, go to the page explaining that stitch.

3 When your beadwork is completed, secure and cut your thread; see instructions on page 28.

4 There are several ways you can finish up your project. Find all our ideas in part 6, beginning on page 166.

RAINDROPS 1 AND 2

Part 2

Part 1

Size: 1⅞ × 11/16 in. (4.8 × 2.6 cm)

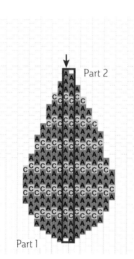

Part 2

Part 1

Size: 19/16 × ⅞ in. (3.9 × 2.1 cm)

Beads of rain

Raining beads

Color Key

DB-1780   DB-2285

DB-2122   DB-0792

A: DB-1780 (Flame Red)
B: DB-2285 (Matte Banana)
C: DB-2122 (Turquoise)
D: DB-0792 (Shale)

RAINDROPS 3 AND 4

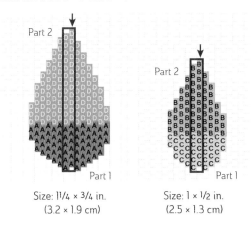

Size: 1¼ × ¾ in.
(3.2 × 1.9 cm)

Size: 1 × ½ in.
(2.5 × 1.3 cm)

RAINDROPS 5 AND 6

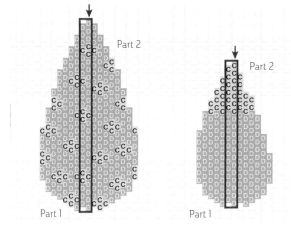

Size: 1¹¹/₁₆ × ⅞ in. (4.3 × 2.2 cm)

Size: 1¼ × ¹¹/₁₆ in. (3.2 × 1.7 cm)

RAINDROPS 7 AND 8

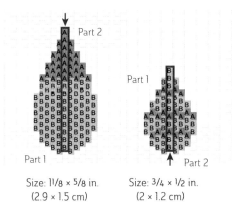

Size: 1⅛ × ⅝ in.
(2.9 × 1.5 cm)

Size: ¾ × ½ in.
(2 × 1.2 cm)

IN WINTER

Autumn is a melancholic and graceful andante that
beautifully makes ready the solemn adagio of winter.
—George Sand

It is up to us—when we have nothing, when everything is slipping away—to give our
life the patience of a work of art, the flexibility of reeds ruffled by the wind's fingers,
in honor of winter. A little silence will suffice.
—Christian Bobin, *The Eighth Day of the Week*

More and more I see winter as the season of introspection and calm—a time that nourishes and prepares for the spring explosion. Each season is useful and necessary. To live them fully, with all our senses, but also in a more philosophical or spiritual way, is to learn to better appreciate the cycles of life and our own life. The patterns I have put in this section are related to Christmas but also to the moon and the stars, to frost, and to the warmth that the home (or baking!) can represent.

BRING YOUR BEADWORK TO LIFE

These patterns can decorate
your tree, gifts, or the house.
They can also find their place on
your Christmas table, decorating
the menu or the napkin rings,
for example. Finally, they can be
worn as a pin, necklace, bracelet,
or earrings. To transform your
beadwork into accessories,
go to page 166.

FIR TREES AND FROSTED LEAVES ★★★☆

Difficult stitches used:
- multiple decrease at beginning of row (see page 22)
- isolated bead (see page 26)
- repositioning the thread (see page 27)

1 Choose your starting method and follow the sequence of stitching as indicated on the chart.

2 To complete any difficult stitch, go to the page explaining that stitch. There are no significant difficulties in these three designs, but due to the many short rows, the thread must be repositioned several times.

3 When your beadwork is completed, secure and cut your thread; see instructions on page 28.

4 There are several ways you can finish up your project. Find all our ideas in part 6, beginning on page 166.

FROSTED LEAF AND SNOWY FIR TREE

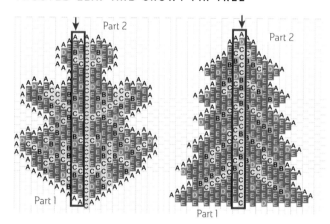

Size: 1⁹/₁₆ × 1¹/₄ in. (3.9 × 3.3 cm)   Size: 1¹/₂ × 1¹/₄ in. (3.8 × 3.3 cm)

Color Key

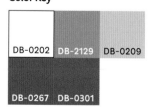

DB-0202   DB-2129   DB-0209

DB-0267   DB-0301

A: DB-0202 (White Pearl)
B: DB-2129 (Moody Blue)
C: DB 0209 (Light Gray)
D: DB-0267 (Blueberry Luster)
E: DB-0301 (Matte Gunmetal)

CHRISTMAS TREE

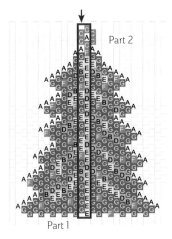

Part 2

Part 1

Size: 1¹¹/₁₆ × 1¹/₄ in. (4.3 × 3.3 cm)

Color Key

DB-0202	DB-1832F	DB-0115	DB-2129
DB-0209	DB-0267	DB-0301	

A: DB-0202 (White Pearl)
B: DB-1832F (Matte Gold)
C: DB-0115 (Dark Topaz Gold)
D: DB-2129 (Moody Blue)
E: DB-0209 (Light Gray)
F: DB-0267 (Blueberry Luster)
G: DB-0301 (Matte Gunmetal)

REINDEER ★★★★

Difficult stitches used:

- multiple decrease at beginning of row (see page 22)
- multiple increase at beginning of row (see page 19)
- multiple increase at end of row (see page 26)
- repositioning the thread (see page 27)

Don't be mistaken—these patterns are reindeer and not deer. Interestingly, both male and female reindeer have antlers, and I like to think that these patterns represent males as well as females.

1 Choose your starting method and follow the sequence of stitching as indicated on the chart. I have not indicated the different parts of the beadwork, because this chart has many discontinuous parts that require the thread to be repositioned many times. These patterns are only for the most experienced bead weavers.

2 To complete any difficult stitch, go to the page explaining that stitch.

3 When your beadwork is completed, secure and cut your thread; see instructions on page 28.

4 There are several ways you can finish up your project. Find all our ideas in part 6, beginning on page 166.

REINDEER HEAD

Size: 1¹/8 × ¹¹/16 in. (2.9 × 1.8 cm)

Color Key

DB-0010	DB-0794	DB-1832F
DB-0115	DB-0211	DB-2129
DB-0209	DB-0267	DB-0301

WHOLE REINDEER

Size: 2¹/16 × 1¹/4 in. (5.2 × 3.3 cm)

A: DB-0010 (Black)
B: DB-0794 (Maple Leaf)
C: DB-1832F (Matte Gold)

D: DB-0115 (Dark Topaz Gold)
E: DB-0211 (Limestone)
F: DB-2129 (Moody Blue)

G: DB-0209 (Light Gray)
H: DB-0267 (Blueberry Luster)
I: DB-0301 (Matte Gunmetal)

– 46 –

CHRISTMAS BOUGH ★★★☆

Difficult stitches used:
- multiple decrease at beginning of row (see page 22)
- repositioning the thread (see page 27)

1 Choose your starting method and follow the sequence of stitching as indicated on the chart.

2 To complete any difficult stitch, go to the page explaining that stitch.

3 When your beadwork is completed, secure and cut your thread; see instructions on page 28.

4 There are several ways you can finish up your project. Find all our ideas in part 6, beginning on page 166.

SPRINGTIME VERSION

Use bright or pastel colors for the flowers and lighter shades of green for the leaves, and this will turn into a lovely springtime pattern! Show me your versions on Instagram by tagging me in your post.

Color Key

DB-2282	DB-1765
DB-0663	
DB-2291	DB-0214
DB-0745	DB-0727

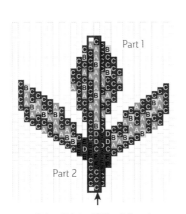

1³⁄8 × 1³⁄8 in. (3.5 × 3.5 cm)

A: DB-2282 (Glazed Smoke)
B: DB-1765 (Celery)
C: DB-0663 (Olive) or DB-2291 (Avocado) for a matte finish
D: DB-0214 (Red Luster)
E: DB-0745 (Matte Transparent Red)
F: DB-0727 (Vermilion Red)

GINGERBREAD HOUSE ★★☆☆

Difficult stitch used: multiple decrease at beginning of row (see page 22)

1 Choose your starting method and follow the sequence of stitching as indicated on the chart.

2 To complete any difficult stitch, go to the page explaining that stitch.

3 When your beadwork is completed, secure and cut your thread; see instructions on page 28.

4 There are several ways you can finish up your project. Find all our ideas in part 6, beginning on page 166.

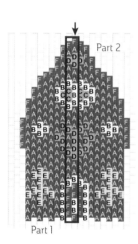

Part 2

Part 1

Size: 1⅝ × 1 in. (4.1 × 2.5 cm)

Color Key

DB-0794	DB-0202
DB-1832F	DB-2129
DB-0209	DB-0301

A: DB-0794 (Maple Leaf)
B: DB-0202 (White Pearl)
C: DB-1832F (Matte Gold)
D: DB-2129 (Moody Blue)
E: DB-0209 (Light Gray)
F: DB-0301 (Matte Gunmetal)

A PAIR OF HORNED OWLS ★★☆☆

Difficult stitch used: multiple decrease at beginning of row (see page 22)

In addition to the owls on page 36, here is a pair of horned owls. Did you know that not all owls are the same? Horned owls have small tufts of feathers resembling ears that other owls do not have.

1 Choose your starting method and follow the sequence of stitching as indicated on the chart.

2 To complete any difficult stitch, go to the page explaining that stitch.

3 When your beadwork is completed, secure and cut your thread; see instructions on page 28.

4 There are several ways you can finish up your project. Find all our ideas in part 6, beginning on page 166.

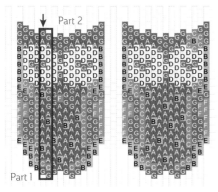

Size: 1 3/8 × 3/4 in. (3.5 × 2 cm)

Color Key

DB-0794	DB-1832F	DB-0115	DB-0211
DB-2129	DB-0267	DB-0301	

A: DB-0794 (Maple Leaf)
B: DB-1832F (Matte Gold)
C: DB-0115 (Dark Topaz Gold)
D: DB-0211 (Limestone)
E: DB-2129 (Moody Blue)
F: DB-0267 (Blueberry Luster)
G: DB-0301 (Matte Gunmetal)

GEOMETRIC DESIGNS

Difficult stitch used (for designs 1 to 3): multiple decrease at beginning of row (see page 22)

1 Choose your starting method and follow the sequence of stitching as indicated on the chart.

2 To complete any difficult stitch, go to the page explaining that stitch. There are no difficult parts in designs 4 and 5.

3 When your beadwork is completed, secure and cut your thread; see instructions on page 28.

4 There are several ways you can finish up your project. Find all our ideas in part 6, beginning on page 166.

DESIGN 1 ★★☆☆

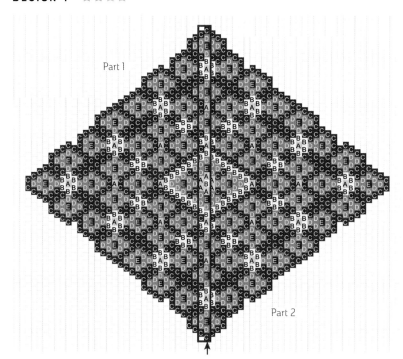

Part 1

Part 2

Size: 2³/4 × 3¹/4 in. (7 × 8.2 cm)

NOTE

The three small designs could become pretty necklaces or bracelets. To do this, add one isolated bead on both the left and the right sides of designs 4 and 5 where you can slide in your jump rings.

Color Key

		DB-2358	DB-2313
DB-1832	DB-1510	DB-0663	DB-2127	DB-0214

A: DB-1832 (Gold)
B: DB-1510 (Bisque White)
C: DB-2358 (Evergreen) or DB-0663 (Olive)
D: DB-2313 (Celadon) or DB-2127 (Spruce)
E: DB-0214 (Red Luster)

DESIGN 2 ★★☆☆

Part 1

Part 2

Size: 2¹¹/₁₆ × 2⁵/₁₆ in. (6.8 × 5.9 cm)

DESIGN 3 ★★☆☆

Part 1

Part 2

Size: ⅝ × ¾ in. (1.5 × 2 cm)

DESIGN 4 ★☆☆☆

Part 1

Part 2

Size: ¾ × ⅞ in. (1.9 × 2.2 cm)

DESIGN 5 ★☆☆☆

Part 1

Part 2

Size: ¾ × ¹¹/₁₆ in. (1.9 × 1.8 cm)

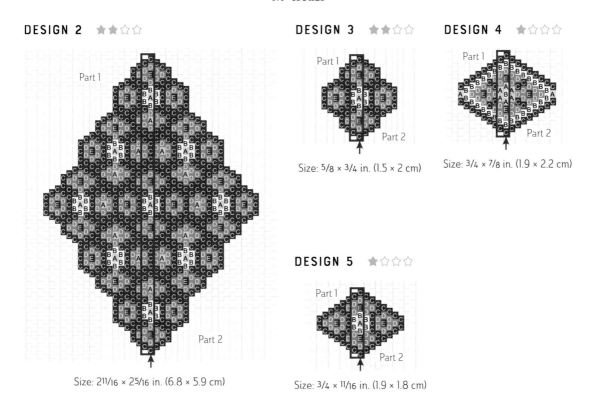

TALISMANS AND GOOD LUCK CHARMS

I give to my hope my heart, as an offering to God. I give to my hope all of the future that trembles like a small glow far off in the forest.
—Guillaume Apollinaire, *Poems to Lou*

Honesty, sincerity, simplicity, humility, generosity, absence of vanity, the ability to serve others—qualities within the reach of all souls— are the true foundations of our spiritual life.
—Nelson Mandela

The notion of spirituality has intrigued me since I was very young. I have read a lot of different things on this subject that have nourished me and helped me grow. In this section, I wanted to talk about something that fascinates me in particular: the form that spirituality can take when it is materialized in a personal object. From the ex-voto (a gift made to God to express gratitude) to the simple lucky charm (by way of symbols showing open-mindedness or talismans having no useful function, not even of being simple decorative elements), these little objects in some way convey our link to the infinitesimal and the tenuous, thus becoming infinitely precious.

BRING YOUR BEADWORK TO LIFE

These designs can be worn as pins (except for the Scarab), but I imagine them more for decoration (frame, embroidery hoop) or to embellish pouches, bags, or notebooks. To transform your beadwork into accessories, go to page 166.

EX-VOTO

Difficult stitches used:

- multiple decrease at beginning of row (see page 22)
- repositioning the thread (see page 27)
- isolated bead (see page 26)
- multiple increase at beginning of row (just for Ex-Voto 2; see page 19)
- multiple increase at end of row (just for Ex-Voto 2; see page 26)

The ex-voto, a symbolic object hung in a church or venerated place as an act of gratitude for some grace received, can take the form of a flaming heart or a sacred heart.

For general steps, see page 56 (disregard references to scarab parts).

EX-VOTO 1 ★★★☆

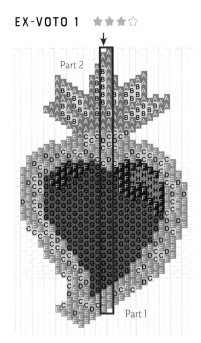

Size: 2⁷/₁₆ × 1¹/₂ in. (6.2 × 3.8 cm)

Color Key

DB-0115	DB-2186	DB-1768	DB-0280
DB-0829	DB-1484	DB-1262	DB-1016

A: DB-0115 (Dark Topaz Gold)
B: DB-2186 (Straw Yellow)
C: DB-0829 (Pale Moss)
D: DB-1484 (Transparent Light Moss Green)
E: DB-1768 (Forest Green)
F: DB-0280 (Cranberry Luster)
G: DB-1262 (Matte Cranberry)
H: DB-1016 (Metallic Rhubarb)

EX-VOTO 2 ★★★★

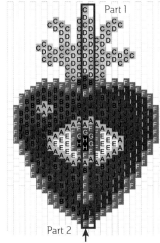

Size: 2 × 1¹/₄ in. (5.1 × 3.3 cm)

Color Key

DB-0235	DB-1780	DB-0651
DB-0042	DB-0066	DB-2381
DB-0306	DB-0010	DB-0214
DB-0727		

A: DB-0235 (Salmon)
B: DB-1780 (Flame Red)
C: DB-0651 (Squash)
D: DB-0042 (Gold)
E: DB-0066 (Bright White)
F: DB-2381 (Inside-Lined Blue Spruce)
G: DB-0306 (Charcoal)
H: DB-0010 (Black)
I: DB-0214 (Red Luster)
J: DB-0727 (Vermilion Red)

If you don't have all the shades of green and red, just use one reference for each color. The result will be less detailed but just as pretty.

LUCKY EYE

Difficult stitches used:

- multiple decrease at beginning of row (see page 22)
- repositioning the thread (except for Lucky Eye 1; see page 27)
- special stitch: add three beads together (except for Lucky Eye 1; see instructions below)
- isolated bead (only for Lucky Eye 3; see page 26)

To complete the special stitch (circled in red), position your thread to come out of the gold bead circled in blue. Pick up three gold beads, and then pass your needle through the first one (the one closest to the beadwork) and pull the thread all the way to the end. To attach this little triangle to the beadwork, pass the needle through the bead circled in green. Reposition your thread in the beads and continue working.

For general steps, see page 56 (disregard references to scarab parts).

Color Key

DB-0200	DB-1832	DB-2186
DB-1005	DB-2144	

A: DB-0200 (White)
B: DB-1832 (Gold)
C: DB-2186 (Straw Yellow)
D: DB-1005 (Metallic Peacock Blue)
E: DB-2144 (Matte French Navy)

LUCKY EYE 1 ★★☆☆

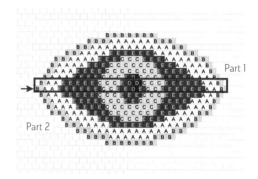

Size: 1 × 1³/₈ in. (2.5 × 3.5 cm)

LUCKY EYE 2 ★★★☆

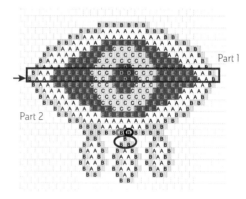

Size: 1⁷/₁₆ × 1³/₈ in. (3.6 × 3.5 cm)

LUCKY EYE 3 ★★★☆

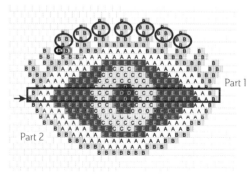

Size: 1¹/₄ × 1³/₈ in. (3.2 × 3.5 cm)

SCARAB ★★★★

Difficult stitches used:
- multiple decrease at beginning of row (see page 22)
- multiple increase at beginning of row (see page 19)
- multiple increase at end of row (see page 26)
- repositioning the thread (see page 27)

Everything ends so that everything begins again, everything dies so that everything lives.
—Jean-Henri Fabre, *Souvenirs Entomologiques*

This pattern is a tribute to the entomologist Jean-Henri Fabre, in memory of how I felt when visiting his house, which has become a magnificent museum-garden (Harmas de Jean-Henri Fabre in Sérignan-du-Comtat in Vaucluse, https://www.harmasjeanhenrifabre.fr).

There are two possible ways to stitch the legs of the beetle:
– Stitch the legs on with the brick stich method (as for the body). You will have to be patient, because it is a real technical challenge.
– Sew the pattern without legs onto your choice of backing, and embroider the legs with beads directly onto the fabric.

1 Choose your starting method and follow the sequence of stitching as indicated on the chart.

2 To complete any difficult stitch, go to the page explaining that stitch. There is only one difficult stitch required for the body of the scarab: the multiple decrease at the beginning of a row. All the other stitches mentioned above are in the legs.

3 When your beadwork is completed, secure and cut your thread; see instructions on page 28.

4 There are several ways you can finish up your project. Find all our ideas in part 6, beginning on page 166.

Size: 3⅝ × 3 in. (9.2 × 7.5 cm)

Color Key

DB-2120	DB-0202	DB-2274
	DB-1765	
	DB-1815	
DB-0203	DB-0357	DB-1170
DB-0002		
DB-1005	DB-0243	DB-1785
DB-0310	DB-2144	DB-0183
DB-0726	DB-2288	

A: DB-2120 (Maroon)
B: DB-0202 (White Pearl)
C: DB-2274 (Glazed Persimmon)
D: DB-0203 (Cream Ceylon)
E: DB-1765 (Celery) or DB-1815 (Pale Lime) or even DB-0357 (Pale Blue Gray)
F: DB-1170 (Matte Aloe Green)
G: DB-0002 (Metallic Dark Blue) or DB-1005 (Metallic Peacock Blue)
H: DB-0243 (Blue Ceylon)
I: DB-1785 (Cobalt Blue)
J: DB-0310 (Matte Black)
K: DB-2144 (Matte French Navy)
L: DB-0183 (Silver-Lined Royal Blue)
M: DB-0726 (Cobalt)
N: DB-2288 (Sienna)

FOR MY BABCIA

My maternal grandfather and my maternal grandmother's parents were Polish immigrants. In my grandmother's house (my "babcia" in Polish), there were many things that reminded us of our family's origins. I remember, for example, the paper cutout pictures, a typical Polish folk art technique, which consists of forming designs from the meticulous cutting of different papers. This art developed in the middle of the nineteenth century in central and eastern Poland and still has a large presence in Polish homes today.

From the Polish folklore of my childhood, I also remember the traditional costumes embroidered with colorful flowers that I wore with great pride.

BRING YOUR BEADWORK TO LIFE

The first patterns in this section have been created from the same color palette so they will match when framed together, sewn onto an embroidery hoop, attached to a pouch or clutch, or glued to a notebook cover. Like the cat designs at the end of the section, they can also be used individually to make pins, necklaces, bracelets, and so forth. To transform your beadwork projects into accessories, go to page 166.

ORANGE FLOWER ★★★★

Difficult stitches used:
- multiple decrease at beginning of row (see page 22)
- multiple increase at beginning of row (see page 19)
- multiple increase at end of row (see page 26)
- repositioning the thread (see page 27)
- special stitch: add three beads together

1 Choose your starting method and follow the sequence of stitching as indicated on the chart.

Part 1: Stitch on the beads continuing in the pattern after the starting row or rows.

Part 2: Start working with your second starting thread, adding on the bottom leaf.

Part 3: Reposition your thread to weave on the very end of the stem.

Part 4: Reposition your thread in the Gunmetal gray bead in front of the part circled in red, and use the special stitch to add the three beads. Pick up three green beads, and then pass your needle through the first one (the one closest to the weave) and pull the thread through to the end. To attach this little triangle to the completed stem, pass the needle through the blue bead. Then bring the needle out through the green bead at the top, which will allow you to resume the pattern by making a simple increase.

Part 5: Reposition the thread to add the left leaf.

Part 6: Reposition the thread to add the left part of the flower.

2 To complete any difficult stitch, go to the page explaining that stitch.

3 When your beadwork is completed, secure and cut your thread; see instructions on page 28.

4 There are several ways you can finish up your project. Find all our ideas in part 6, beginning on page 166.

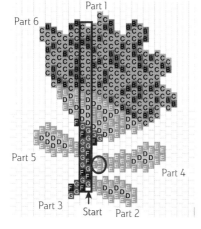

Size: 1³/4 × 1¹/4 in. (4.4 × 3.2 cm)

Color Key

DB-0116	DB-1133	DB-0651
DB-0374	DB-0264	DB-0183
DB-0301	DB-0362	DB-2308

A: DB-0116 (Wine Luster)
B: DB-1133 (Mandarin)
C: DB-0651 (Squash)
D: DB-0374 (Matte Sea Foam)
E: DB-0264 (Mallard Luster)
F: DB-0183 (Silver-Lined Royal Blue)
G: DB-0301 (Matte Gunmetal)
H: DB-0362 (Red Luster)
I: DB-2308 (Merlot)

The colors in this color chart apply to all patterns in this section (except for the Cats).

BLUE BIRDS

Difficult stitches used:
- multiple decrease at beginning of row (see page 22)
- multiple increase at beginning of row (see page 19)
- multiple increase at end of row (for Bird with Large Tail only; see page 26)
- repositioning the thread (see page 27)
- isolated bead (see page 26)

1 Choose your starting method and follow the sequence of stitching as indicated on the chart.

2 To complete any difficult stitch, go to the page explaining that stitch.

3 When your beadwork is completed, secure and cut your thread; see instructions on page 28.

4 There are several ways you can finish up your project. Find all our ideas in part 6, beginning on page 166.

BLUE BIRD WITH LARGE TAIL

★★★★

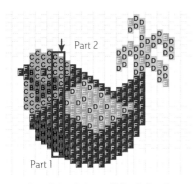

Size: 1³/8 × 1⁷/16 in. (3.5 × 3.6 cm)

BLUE BIRD WITH SMALL TAIL

★★★☆

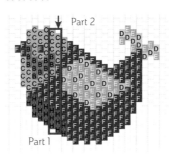

Size: 1¹/16 × 1⁵/16 in. (2.6 × 3.4 cm)

For Color Key, please refer
to the color chart on page 60.

SINGLE PINK AND ORANGE FLOWER ★★★★

Difficult stitches used:
- multiple decrease at beginning of row (see page 22)
- multiple increase at end of row (see page 26)
- repositioning the thread (see page 27)

1 If you are very comfortable with bead weaving, you can complete the different parts of the pattern in the order that you find most convenient for you. If not, here's how to understand the different steps shown in the chart.

Part 1: After stitching the two starting rows, start with P1 and work 5 continuous rows.

Part 2: You then arrive at the area circled in red. Stitch the two small rows of two beads marked "P2."

Part 3: Then reposition your thread to add on P3.

Part 4: Add a new thread to begin P4 at the point indicated by the P4 arrow. Stitch continuously until the flower is finished.

Part 5: Resume stitching at P5 (with your starting thread if you started with two rows) and complete the last row.

Part 6: Attach the flower to the stem by passing a thread through the beadwork.

2 To complete any difficult stitch, go to the page explaining that stitch.

3 When your beadwork is completed, secure and cut your thread; see instructions on page 28.

4 There are several ways you can finish up your project. Find all our ideas in part 6, beginning on page 166.

> ## NOTE
> These patterns are complex because there are many indented parts and gaps without beads in the patterns.

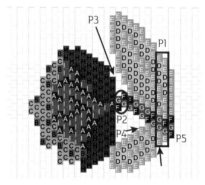

Size: 1⁷/₁₆ × 1⁵/₁₆ in. (3.6 × 3.4 cm)

For Color Key, please refer to the color chart on page 60.

DOUBLE PINK AND ORANGE FLOWER ★★★★

Difficult stitches used:

- multiple decrease at beginning of row (see page 22)
- multiple increase at end of row (see page 26)
- repositioning the thread (see page 27)

If you are very comfortable with bead weaving, you can complete the different parts of the pattern in the order that you find most convenient for you. If not, here's how to understand the different steps shown in the chart.

Part 1: After stitching the two starting rows, start with P1 and work seven continuous rows. You then arrive at the area circled in red.

Part 2: Stitch the two small rows of two beads marked "P2."

Part 3: Then reposition your thread to add on P3.

Part 4: Add a new thread to begin P4 at the point indicated by the P4 arrow. Stitch continuously until the flower is finished.

Part 5: Resume stitching at P5 and work six continuous rows. You then arrive at the area circled in red.

Part 6: Stitch the two small rows of two beads marked "P6."

Part 7: Then reposition your thread to add on P7.

Part 8: To start on P8, place a new thread at the point indicated by the arrow. Stitch continuously until the flower is finished.

Part 9: When both of your flowers are finished, attach each of them to the stem by passing a thread through the beadwork.

For the general steps, see opposite page.

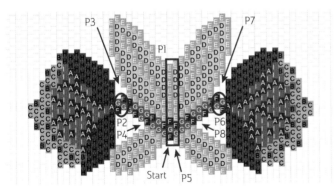

Size: 2⅝ × 1⁷⁄₁₆ in. (6.6 × 3.6 cm)

For Color Key, please refer to the color chart on page 60.

BLUE FLOWERS ★★★☆

Difficult stitches used:
- multiple decrease at beginning of row (see page 22)
- multiple increase at end of row (see page 26)
- repositioning the thread (see page 27)
- isolated bead (only for the Small Blue Flower; see page 26)

1 Choose your starting method and follow the sequence of stitching, completing the parts as indicated on the chart.

For the Large Flower

Part 1: Stitch on beads continuing in the pattern after the starting row or rows. If you started with two rows, you must first add a bead at the end of the row.

Part 2: Position the thread so that you can restart your stitching at the point indicated by the arrow, and then work the rest of the flower.

Part 3: Reposition your thread to stitch on the left leaf.

Part 4: Use your second starting thread to stitch on the right leaf.

For the Small Flower

To simplify the weaving, start with two rows; this will allow you to avoid multiple increases, which are necessary with a one-row start.

Part 1: Stitch the left part in continuous rows from the starting rows.

Part 2: Start this part with your second starting thread and stitch in continuous rows until the end of the right leaf.

Part 3: Reposition the thread at the point indicated by the arrow to stitch the end of the flower.

2 To complete any difficult stitch, go to the page explaining that stitch.

3 When your beadwork is completed, secure and cut your thread; see instructions on page 28.

4 There are several ways you can finish up your project. Find all our ideas in part 6, beginning on page 166.

LARGE BLUE FLOWER

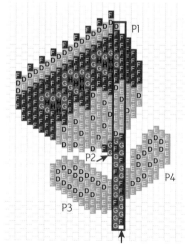

Size: 1 7/8 × 1 1/2 in. (4.8 × 3.8 cm)

SMALL BLUE FLOWER

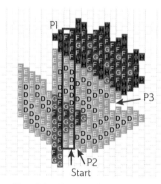

Size: 1 1/4 × 1 3/16 in. (3.3 × 3 cm)

For Color Key, please refer to the color chart on page 60.

SMALL LEAF ★★☆☆

Difficult stitches used:
- multiple decrease at beginning of row (see page 22)—if starting with 1 row
- multiple increase at end of row (see page 26)—if starting with 2 rows
- repositioning the thread (see page 27)

1 Choose your starting method and follow the sequence of the stitching, as indicated on the chart. To simplify things, start with one row. If you start with two rows, you must add a bead at the end of your starting row. To do this, position your thread in the row to be increased and proceed as with a multiple increase at the end of the row (see page 26). Then replace the thread from the other side to start to work Part 1.

2 To complete any difficult stitch, go to the page explaining that stitch.

3 When your beadwork is completed, secure and cut your thread; see instructions on page 28.

4 There are several ways you can finish up your project. Find all our ideas in part 6, beginning on page 166.

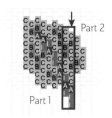

Size: 3/4 × 5/8 in. (1.9 × 1.5 cm)

For Color Key, please refer to the color chart on page 60.

PINK BIRD ★★★★

Difficult stitches used:
- multiple decrease at beginning of row (see page 22)
- multiple increase at beginning of row (see page 19)
- multiple increase at end of row (see page 26)
- isolated bead (see page 26)

1 Choose your starting method and follow the sequence of the stitching, as indicated on the chart. If you start with two rows, you must add a bead at the end of your starting row. To do this, position your thread in the row to be increased and proceed as with a multiple increase at end of row (see page 26).

2 To complete any difficult stitch, go to the page explaining that stitch.

3 When your beadwork is completed, secure and cut your thread; see instructions on page 28.

4 There are several ways you can finish up your project. Find all our ideas in part 6, beginning on page 166.

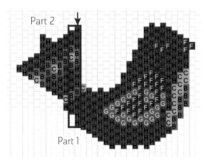

Size: 1¹/8 × 1⁹/16 in. (2.9 × 4 cm)

For Color Key, please refer to the color chart on page 60.

LITTLE CATS

Difficult stitches used:
- multiple decrease at beginning of row (see page 22)
- multiple increase at end of row (see page 26)

The ideal of calm exists in a sitting cat. —Jules Renard, *Journal*

I made two versions of this pattern: with or without little front legs, the first being more difficult than the other.

1 Choose your starting method and follow the sequence of stitching as indicated on the chart.

2 To complete any difficult stitch, go to the page explaining that stitch.

TIP

To simplify this pattern as much as possible, I suggest that when Part 2 is completed, you replace the thread with a new one in order to restart stitching at Part 3.

3 When your beadwork is completed, secure and cut your thread; see instructions on page 28.

4 There are several ways you can finish up your project. Find all our ideas in part 6, beginning on page 166.

LITTLE CAT WITH 2 LEGS ★★★★

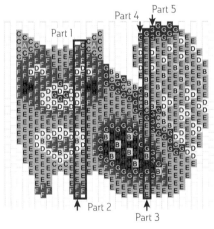

Size: 1⁹⁄₁₆ × 1³⁄₄ in. (4 × 4.4 cm)

LITTLE CAT WITHOUT LEGS ★★★☆

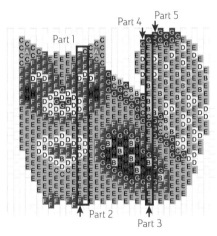

Size: 1⁹⁄₁₆ × 1³⁄₄ in. (4 × 4.4 cm)

Color Key

DB-1779	DB-1832	DB-2106	DB-0732
DB-0759	DB-0301	DB-0002	DB-0874

A: DB-1779 (Caramel)
B: DB-1832 (Gold)
C: DB-2106 (Hawthorne)
D: DB-0732 (Dark Cream)
E: DB-0759 (Turquoise)
F: DB-0301 (Matte Gunmetal)
G: DB-0002 (Metallic Dark Blue)
H: DB-0874 (Red Pink)

LARGE CATS

Difficult stitches used:
- multiple decrease at beginning of row (see page 22)
- multiple increase at end of row (see page 26)

As for the little cats, I made two versions of the pattern for the side view of the large cat: with or without little front legs. The version without the legs contains fewer complex stitches than the other.

1 Choose your starting method and follow the sequence of stitching as indicated on the chart.

2 To complete any difficult stitch, go to the page explaining that stitch.

3 When your beadwork is completed, secure and cut your thread; see instructions on page 28.

4 There are several ways you can finish up your project. Find all our ideas in part 6, beginning on page 166.

LARGE CAT SIDE VIEW WITHOUT LEGS ★★★☆

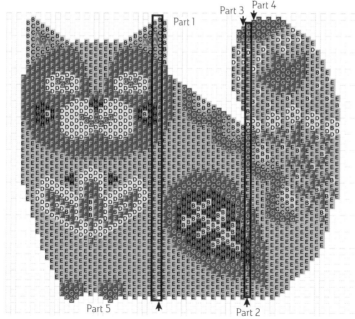

Part 3 Part 4
Part 1
Part 5 Part 2

For Color Key, please refer to the color chart on page 67.

Size: 3 × 3½ in. (7.5 × 8.5 cm)

LARGE CAT SIDE VIEW WITH LEGS ★★★★

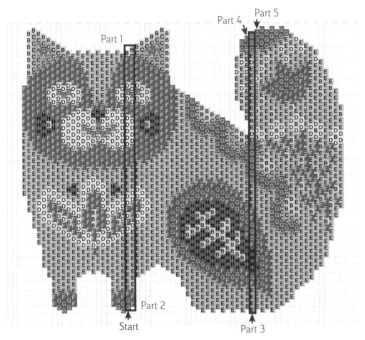

Part 4   Part 5
Part 1
Part 2
Start
Part 3

> ### TIP
>
> To simplify these patterns, I suggest that when Part 2 of the Large Cat Side View with Legs or Part 3 of the Large Cat Side View without Legs is completed, replace the thread with a new one before moving on to the next indicated part.

Size: 3 × 3½ in. (7.5 × 8.5 cm)

LARGE CAT FRONT VIEW ★★☆☆

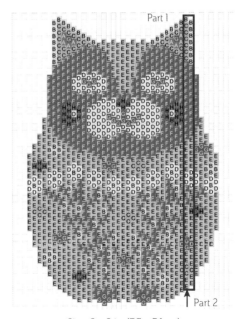

Part 1

Part 2

Size: 3 × 2 in. (7.5 × 5.1 cm)

FLOWERS, FLOWERS, FLOWERS!

The flowers of spring are the dreams of winter told,
in the morning, at the table of angels.
—Gibran Khalil Gibran

And for you I will be a child working the fields,
who makes his land grow to offer you his flowers.
—Barbara, from the album *Les Insomnies*

•◦•

Ah, flowers! Gifts of nature, gifts of life, gifts of love! I love them all, the ones in my garden, the ones in the fields (even if we see fewer and fewer of them on the roadside, unfortunately), the ones we offer in bouquets, but also the ones we see in painters' works, in writers' and poets' books, and in children's drawings. My love for flowers is immense; they have all my gratitude.

BRING YOUR BEADWORK TO LIFE

Most of the designs in this section can be worn as necklaces or pins, but they can also be sewn or glued on anything. The smaller designs, like the Mini Flowers, can be used to make beautiful earrings. To transform your beadwork into accessories, go to page 166.

SMALL BOUQUETS ★★★☆

Difficult stitches used:

- multiple decrease at beginning of row (see page 22)
- multiple increase at end of row (see page 26)
- isolated bead (see page 26)
- repositioning the thread (see page 27)

1 Choose your starting method and follow the sequence of stitching as indicated on the chart.

2 To complete any difficult stitch, go to the page explaining that stitch.

3 When your beadwork is completed, secure and cut your thread; see instructions on page 28.

4 There are several ways you can finish up your project. Find all our ideas in part 6, beginning on page 166.

PINK BOUQUET

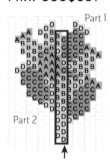

Part 1

Part 2

Size: 1 1/8 × 3/4 in. (2.8 × 2 cm)

Color Key

| DB-2114 | DB-1495 |
| DB-2178 | DB-0411 |

A: DB-2114 (Light Watermelon)
B: DB-1495 (Pink Champagne)
C: DB-2178 (Papaya)
D: DB-0411 (Gold)

GREEN BOUQUET

Size: 1 1/8 × 3/4 in. (2.8 × 2 cm)

Color Key

| DB-2178 | DB-0411 | DB-2291 |
| DB-2282 | DB-2052 | |

A: DB-2178 (Papaya)
B: DB-0411 (Gold)
C: DB-2282 (Glazed Smoke)
D: DB-2052 (Asparagus Green)
E: DB-2291 (Avocado)

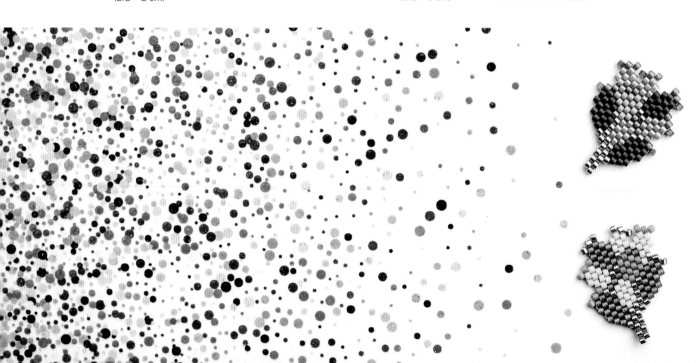

FORGET-ME-NOTS

Difficult stitches used:

- multiple decrease at beginning of row (see page 22)
- multiple increase at end of row (only for Bouquet pattern; see page 26)
- repositioning the thread (see page 27)

These forget-me-not flowers are composed of a gradient of five shades of blue. I also chose different bead finishes (shiny, matte, etc.) to play on the depth and the effects of the pattern with the light. This is the perfect pattern to understand how to create gradients and reflections that enhance the beadwork. I invite you to try re-creating this effect in other colors. Show me your versions on Instagram by tagging me in your post!

For general steps, see page 72.

FORGET-ME-NOT
★★☆☆☆

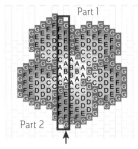

Size: 15/16 × 1 in. (3.4 × 2.5 cm)

FORGET-ME-NOT BOUQUET
★★★☆☆

Size: 15/8 × 15/8 in. (4.1 × 4.1 cm)

Color Key

DB-0200	DB-2186	DB-0239
DB-0628	DB-0375	
DB-1783	DB-2135	

A: DB-0200 (White)
B: DB-2186 (Straw Yellow)
C: DB-0239 (Light Aqua Ceylon)
D: DB-0628 (Aqua Blue)
E: DB-0375 (Turquoise Blue)
F: DB-1783 (Capri Blue)
G: DB-2135 (Juniper Berry)

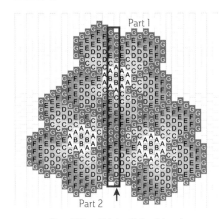

MINI FLOWERS

Difficult stitches used for Patterns 1 and 2:
- multiple decrease at beginning of row (see page 22)
- multiple increase at end of row (only for Pattern 1; see page 26)
- repositioning the thread (see page 27)

This pattern is available in several colors and in three versions: Pattern 1, more broken up, has a little more complex stitching than Pattern 2. Pattern 3, with no stem or leaves, has no difficult stitches.

1 Choose your starting method and follow the sequence of the stitching, completing the parts as indicated on the chart.

2 To complete any difficult stitch, go to the page explaining that stitch.

3 When your beadwork is completed, secure and cut your thread; see instructions on page 28.

4 There are several ways you can finish up your project. Find all our ideas in part 6, beginning on page 166.

PATTERN 1 ★★★☆

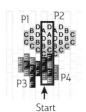

Start

Size: 9/16 × 1/2 in. (1.4 × 1.3 cm)

Color Key

DB-1831		
DB-0551	DB-0160	DB-2283
DB-0232	DB-2310	DB-0663

A: DB-1831 (Galvanized Silver)
or DB-0551 (Bright Silver)
for a silver without yellow
highlights
B: DB-0160 (Dark Yellow)
C: DB-2283 (Citron)
D: DB-0232 (Light Lemon)
E: DB-2310 (Pistachio)
F: DB-0663 (Olive)

PATTERN 2 ★★☆☆

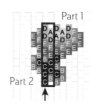

Part 1

Part 2

Size: 9/16 × 1/2 in. (1.4 × 1.2 cm)

Color Key

DB-1152	DB-2310	DB-0663
DB-2129	DB-2384	DB-2132

A: DB-1152 (Matte Gold)
B: DB-2310 (Pistachio)
C: DB-0663 (Olive)
D: DB-2129 (Moody Blue)
E: DB-2384 (Teal Dark Blue)
F: DB-2132 (Bayberry)

PATTERN 3 ★☆☆☆

Part 1

Part 2

Size: 5/16 × 1/2 in. (0.8 × 1.2 cm)

Color Key

DB-1152	DB-2129
DB-2384	DB-2132

A: DB-1152 (Matte Gold)
B: DB-2129 (Moody Blue)
C: DB-2384 (Teal Dark Blue)
D: DB-2132 (Bayberry)

Flowers, Flowers, Flowers!

BLUE VERSION

Size: 9/16 × 1/2 in.
(1.4 × 1.3 cm)

Color Key

DB-0040	DB-2310	DB-0663
DB-1785	DB-2143	DB-0183

A: DB-0040 (Copper)
B: DB-2310 (Pistachio)
C: DB-0663 (Olive)
D: DB-1785 (Cobalt Blue)
E: DB-2143 (Navy)
F: DB-0183 (Silver-Lined Royal Blue)

PINK VERSION

Size: 9/16 × 1/2 in.
(1.4 × 1.3 cm)

Color Key

DB-1363	DB-1523	DB-1156
DB-1152	DB-2310	DB-0663

A: DB-1363 (Pink Grapefruit)
B: DB-1523 (Light Salmon)
C: DB-1156 (Blush)
D: DB-1152 (Matte Gold)
E: DB-2310 (Pistachio)
F: DB-0663 (Olive)

BURGUNDY VERSION

Size: 9/16 × 1/2 in.
(1.4 × 1.3 cm)

Color Key

DB-0116	DB-0040	DB-2310
DB-0663	DB-1565	DB-1584

A: DB-0116 (Wine Luster)
B: DB-0040 (Copper)
C: DB-2310 (Pistachio)
D: DB-0663 (Olive)
E: DB-1565 (Currant Luster)
F: DB-1584 (Matte Currant)

RED VERSION

Size: 9/16 × 1/2 in.
(1.4 × 1.3 cm)

Color Key

DB-0753	DB-0040	DB-1780
DB-2310	DB-0663	DB-0791

A: DB-0753 (Matte Red)
B: DB-0040 (Copper)
C: DB-1780 (Flame Red)
D: DB-2310 (Pistachio)
E: DB-0663 (Olive)
F: DB-0791 (Lipstick Red)

SMALL SCANDINAVIAN FLOWERS, COMPLEX VERSIONS ★★★★

Difficult stitches used:

- multiple decrease at beginning of row (see page 22)
- multiple increase at beginning of row (see page 19)
- multiple increase at end of row (see page 26)
- repositioning the thread (see page 27)

The first four designs in this series feature tiny red flowers that create cutout areas on the top which are very complex to make. I would therefore only recommend it to the most experienced bead weavers.

1 Choose your starting method and follow the sequence of the stitching, completing the parts as indicated on the charts. To simplify the stitching, I suggest you start with one row.

2 To complete any difficult stitch, go to the page explaining that stitch.

3 When your beadwork is completed, secure and cut your thread; see instructions on page 28.

4 There are several ways you can finish up your project. Find all our ideas in part 6, beginning on page 166.

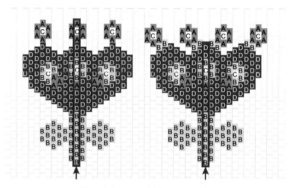

Size: 1⅛ × 1 in. (2.9 × 2.4 cm)

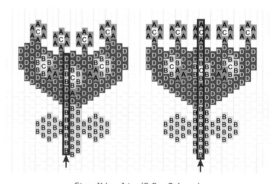

Size: 1⅛ × 1 in. (2.9 × 2.4 cm)

Color Key

| DB-1780 | DB-1832 | DB-1510 | DB-2143 |

A: DB-1780 (Flame Red)
B: DB-1832 (Gold)
C: DB-1510 (Bisque White)
D: DB-2143 (Navy)

SMALL SCANDINAVIAN FLOWERS, SIMPLE VERSIONS ★★☆☆

Difficult stitches used:
- multiple decrease at beginning of row (see page 22)
- repositioning the thread (see page 27)

These three patterns omit the tiny red flowers and are accessible to all, including beginners.

To simplify the stitching, I suggest you start with two rows and complete the parts as indicated on the chart.

Part 1: Stitch where the pattern continues after the starting row or rows. Secure and cut your thread at the end of this part. For the second pattern, the thread must be repositioned once to stitch the left side of the flower and the left leaf.

Part 2: With your second starting thread, stitch Part 2.

Part 3: For the first and third patterns, replace the thread with a new one to stitch on Part 3.

For general steps, see opposite page.

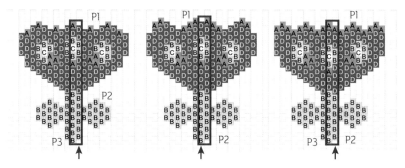

Size: 11/16 × 1 in. (2.7 × 2.4 cm)

For Color Key, please refer to the color chart on page 76.

LARGE SCANDINAVIAN FLOWER ★★★★

Difficult stitches used:
- multiple decrease at beginning of row (see page 22)
- multiple increase at beginning of row (see page 19)
- multiple increase at end of row (see page 26)
- repositioning the thread (see page 27)

This large pattern is perfect to be framed, sewn onto a pouch or bag, or glued to a notebook.

To simplify the stitching, I advise you to start with two rows and to complete the parts in the order shown on the chart.

Part 1: Stitch on beads, continuing in the pattern after the starting row or rows. The stitching will be continuous up to the end of the right or left leaf, depending on the pattern.

Part 2: Reposition the thread to start up again at the point indicated by arrow P2. Stitch a part of the flower (you will need to reposition the thread several times to stitch the top red flower).

Part 3: With your second starting thread, work Part 3 up to the end of the second leaf.

Part 4: Reposition the thread to start up again at the point indicated by arrow P4. Stitch a part of the flower (you will need to reposition the thread several times to stitch the top red flower).

For general steps, see page 76.

For Color Key, please refer to the color chart on page 76.

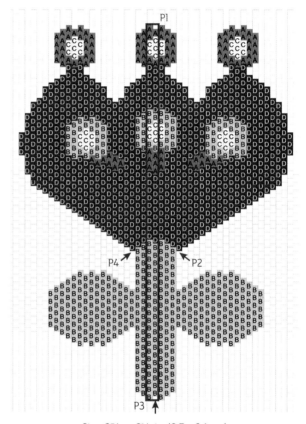

Size: 3⁷/₁₆ × 2¹/₂ in. (8.7 × 6.4 cm)

LILY

Difficult stitches used:
- multiple decrease at beginning of row (see page 22)
- repositioning the thread (see page 27)

1. Choose your starting method and follow the sequence of stitching as indicated on the chart.

2. To complete any difficult stitch, go to the page explaining that stitch.

3. When your beadwork is completed, secure and cut your thread; see instructions on page 28.

4. There are several ways you can finish up your project. Find all our ideas in part 6, beginning on page 166.

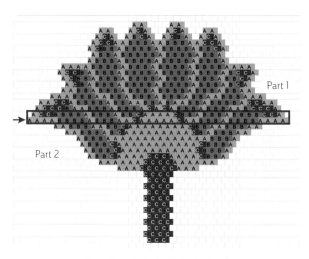

Size: 1⁷/₈ × 2⁵/₁₆ in. (4.8 × 5.9 cm)

Color Key

DB-0243	DB-1597	DB-0277

A: DB-0243 (Blue Ceylon)
B: DB-1597 (Matte Cyan Blue)
C: DB-0277 (Cobalt)

SPRING FLOWER ★★☆☆

Difficult stitches used:
- multiple decrease at beginning of row (see page 22)
- repositioning the thread (see page 27)

As this section winds up, you will find this same floral design placed on a woman's head as a beautiful headdress for women of all colors and ages.

1 Choose your starting method and follow the sequence of stitching as indicated on the chart.

2 To complete any difficult stitch, go to the page explaining that stitch.

3 When your beadwork is completed, secure and cut your thread; see instructions on page 28.

4 There are several ways you can finish up your project. Find all our ideas in part 6, beginning on page 166.

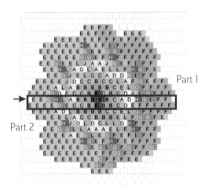

Size: 1 1/4 × 15/16 in. (3.3 × 3.4 cm)

Color Key

DB-0868	DB-2104	DB-0651
DB-1510	DB-0628	DB-0375
DB-0792	DB-2384	DB-2133
DB-0875	DB-0874	DB-0070

A: DB-0868 (Pink Mist)
B: DB-2104 (Kumquat)
C: DB-0651 (Squash)
D: DB-1510 (Bisque White)
E: DB-0628 (Aqua Blue)
F: DB-0375 (Turquoise Blue)
G: DB-0792 (Shale)
H: DB-2384 (Teal Dark Blue)
I: DB-2133 (Dark Azure)
J: DB-0875 (Light Mauve)
K: DB-0874 (Red Pink)
L: DB-0070 (Coral)

FLORAL COMPOSITIONS ★★☆☆

Difficult stitches used:
- multiple decrease at beginning of row (see page 22)
- repositioning the thread (see page 27)

VERSION 1

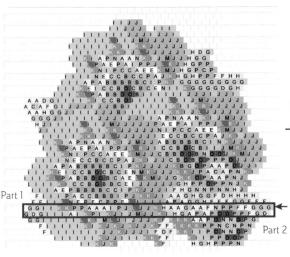

Size: 2 × 2¼ in. (5 × 5.7 cm)

VERSION 2

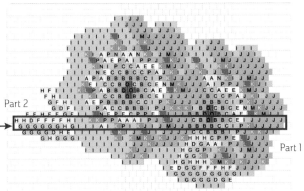

Size: 1⁷⁄₁₆ × 2½ in. (3.6 × 6.3 cm)

Color Key

DB-0868	DB-2104	DB-0651	DB-1831	DB-1510	DB-2283
DB-2309	DB-2123	DB-0628	DB-0375	DB-0792	
DB-2384	DB-2133	DB-0875	DB-0874	DB-0070	

A: DB-0868 (Pink Mist)
B: DB-2104 (Kumquat)
C: DB-0651 (Squash)
D: DB-1831 (Galvanized Silver)
E: DB-1510 (Bisque White)
F: DB-2283 (Citron)
G: DB-2309 (Fern)
H: DB-2123 (Fennel)

I: DB-0628 (Aqua Blue)
J: DB-0375 (Turquoise Blue)
K: DB-0792 (Shale)
L: DB-2384 (Teal Dark Blue)
M: DB-2133 (Dark Azure)
N: DB-0875 (Light Mauve)
O: DB-0874 (Red Pink)
P: DB-0070 (Coral)

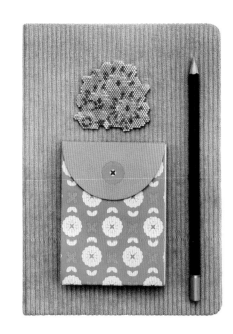

FACE WITH FLORAL HEADDRESS ★★☆☆

Difficult stitches used:
- multiple decrease at beginning of row (see page 22)
- repositioning the thread (see page 27)

1. Choose your starting method and follow the sequence of stitching as indicated on the chart.

2. To complete any difficult stitch, go to the page explaining that stitch.

3. When your beadwork is completed, secure and cut your thread; see instructions on page 28.

4. There are several ways you can finish up your project. Find all our ideas in part 6, beginning on page 166.

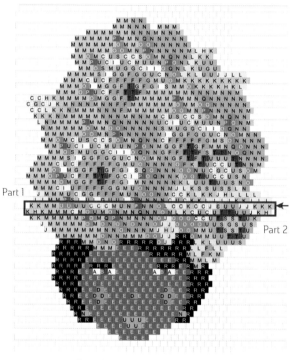

Size: 2³/4 × 2¹/4 in. (7 × 5.7 cm)

Color Key

DB-0066	DB-1779	DB-0868	DB-1790	DB-0769	DB-2104
DB-0651	DB-1831	DB-1510	DB-2283	DB-2309	DB-2123
DB-0628	DB-0375	DB-0792	DB-2384	DB-2133	DB-0310
DB-0875	DB-0874	DB-0070			

A: DB-0066 (Bright White)
To limit the number of colors, you can use the same color for beads A and I (white).

B: DB-1779 (Caramel)
C: DB-0868 (Pink Mist)
D: DB-1790 (Sable)
E: DB-0769 (Matte Root Beer)
F: DB-2104 (Kumquat)
G: DB-0651 (Squash)
H: DB-1831 (Galvanized Silver)
I: DB-1510 (Bisque White)
J: DB-2283 (Citron)
K: DB-2309 (Fern)
L: DB-2123 (Fennel)

M: DB-0628 (Aqua Blue)
N: DB-0375 (Turquoise Blue)
O: DB-0792 (Shale)
P: DB-2384 (Teal Dark Blue)
Q: DB-2133 (Dark Azure)
R: DB-0310 (Matte Black)
S: DB-0875 (Light Mauve)
T: DB-0874 (Red Pink)
U: DB-0070 (Coral)

BUST WITH FLORAL HEADDRESS ★★★★

Difficult stitches used:
- multiple decrease at beginning of row (see page 22)
- multiple increase at beginning of row (see page 19)
- multiple increase at end of row (see page 26)
- repositioning the thread (see page 27)

For general steps, see opposite page.

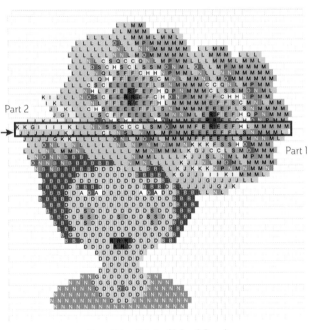

Part 2

Part 1

Size: 2½ × 2½ in. (6.4 × 6.3 cm)

Color Key

DB-0066	DB-0794	DB-0868	DB-0354	DB-2104
DB-0651	DB-1831	DB-1510	DB-2283	DB-2309
DB-2123	DB-0628	DB-0375	DB-0792	DB-2384
DB-2133	DB-0875	DB-0874	DB-0070	

A: DB-0066 (Bright White)

To limit the number of colors, you can use the same color for beads A and H (white).

B: DB-0794 (Maple Leaf)
C: DB-0868 (Pink Mist)
D: DC-0354 (Blush)
E: DB-2104 (Kumquat)
F: DB-0651 (Squash)
G: DB-1831 (Galvanized Silver)
H: DB-1510 (Bisque White)
I: DB-2283 (Citron)
J: DB-2309 (Fern)
K: DB-2123 (Fennel)

L: DB-0628 (Aqua Blue)
M: DB-0375 (Turquoise Blue)
N: DB-0792 (Shale)
O: DB-2384 (Teal Dark Blue)
P: DB-2133 (Dark Azure)
Q: DB-0875 (Light Mauve)
R: DB-0874 (Red Pink)
S: DB-0070 (Coral)

OTHER VARIATIONS

PART 2

PEYOTE STITCH: METHOD AND PATTERNS

In this section, you will find all the instructions to use the peyote method in bead weaving projects.

This method allows you to weave back and forth or in the round. For weaving back and forth, there are two techniques: even-count and odd-count peyote stitch. These two stitches are faster than the brick stitch, but they do not allow for making increases (or only in some cases, and the method is quite complex). We will use them to make bracelets or rings that are rectangular.

For weaving in the round, there are circular, triangular, hexagonal, or pentagonal peyote stitches. Here again, the projects can be completed quickly, and several different geometric shapes can be made: circles, triangles, hexagons, and pentagons, as well as stars!

NOTE

If you are just starting out, you will find all the information concerning the materials and all the general advice on bead weaving in the introduction section (page 8).

Reading a Weaving Chart for Even-Count and Odd-Count Peyote Stitches

Peyote stitch is woven in staggered rows. Each new row is interlocked between the beads of the previous row. Even though this can be hard to read on a chart, the technique is easy.

NOTE

Charts show only even- and odd-count peyote. Written directions are given for circular peyote stitch.

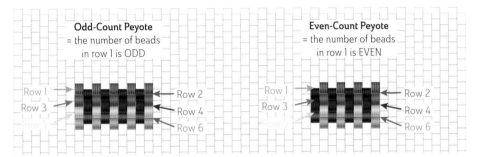

The pattern is woven in one direction and then in the other direction.

For peyote stitch, it is important to know how to distinguish an even-count chart from an odd-count chart; it affects the weaving method used. The number of beads in row 1 indicates which one it is.

1. If this number is even, you must use the even-count peyote stitch method.

2. If this number is odd, you must use the odd-count peyote stitch method.

NOTE

There is an additional difficulty when doing odd-count peyote stitch, as you must move the thread to the right place every other row before being able to start the next one.

EVEN-COUNT AND ODD-COUNT PEYOTE STITCHES

STARTING A PROJECT

With bead weaving, the first few rows are often the hardest. Peyote stitch is no different. Here is the method used to start even-count or odd-count peyote stitch.

To make the first rows easier to stitch, there are "Quick Start Peyote Cards" available in craft stores. I would recommend these to you, particularly if you are just starting out or if you are making a larger-size pattern (like cuffs).

The Three Set-Up Rows (Even-Count and Odd-Count Peyote)

The step-by-step instructions below are based on the following charts.

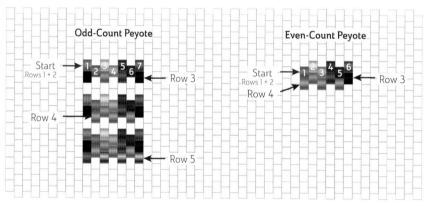

The numbers indicate the order in which you must pick up the first beads.

Prepare your thread (about 2½ feet/80 cm or more) and your needle. Don't knot the end of the thread.

Pick up all the beads in the first two rows in the order indicated. At this stage, the difference between even-count and odd-count peyote stitch is simply the number of beads that you start with.

After sliding on the beads, there should be at least 20–24 in. (50–60 cm) between the beads and your needle.

All the beads in the first two rows must be on the thread when you start, either an even or an odd number, depending on the chart.

Weave the first three rows together, adding the beads in the third row one at a time. For the three brown beads (dark brown, medium brown, and light brown), the method is the same for both even and odd count.

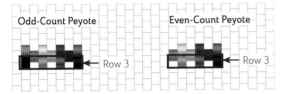

In this odd-count peyote, there are four beads (brown + black) in row 3. In this even-count peyote, there are three beads (brown) in row 3.

Place the beads already picked up over your finger so that the first bead in the row is on the top. Pinch the beads with your thumb so they don't fall off the thread, and pick up the first bead of row 3 (here, the dark brown bead). Then pass the needle through the second bead on the thread (red bead).

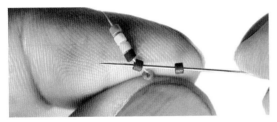

After picking up the first bead of row 3 (dark brown), pass your needle through the red bead.

Pull gently on the thread all the way to the end, making sure not to lose any beads that haven't been woven in yet.

The two beads from the first two rows and the first bead of the third row will fall into a staggered position and form a little triangle.

The remaining two brown beads (medium and light brown) are stitched on in the same way:

- with the medium brown bead on the needle, pass through the pink bead
- with the light brown bead on the needle, pass through the green bead

Important: As you work on row 3, be sure that it does not twist. If it does, turn the beads with your fingers to place them in the right direction.

For even-count peyote, once all the beads from row 3 (brown) are inserted in the weaving, the set-up is completed. You can proceed to the step "Starting a New Row" on the next page.

For odd-count peyote, there is only one bead left on the thread (orange) and the last bead of row 3 to be inserted (black). There is therefore an additional step to complete to attach the bead correctly.

Adding the Last Bead of the Set-Up Rows (Odd-Count Peyote)

To stitch the last bead of row 3 for an odd-count peyote (here, the black bead), pass your needle through the first bead of the starting rows (here, the orange bead).

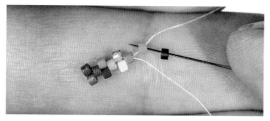

After picking up the black bead, pass your needle through the orange bead going back toward the inside of the weaving.

Your bead is attached. To start row 4, move your thread to the right spot, following the path shown in the diagram below.

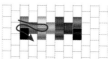

Your thread is now in the right place for you to move on to the "Starting a New Row" step.

STARTING A NEW ROW

Before stitching your new row, find on the chart which situation your own case matches.

First case: The new row contains the same number of beads as the set-up rows. For odd-count peyote, where the set-up rows have a different number of beads, the new row must contain the same number of beads as row 1 or row 2.

Second case: There is a decrease in the new row; it contains fewer beads than the set-up rows. For odd-count peyote, since the set-up rows have a different number of beads, a decrease row must contain fewer beads than the smallest set-up row.

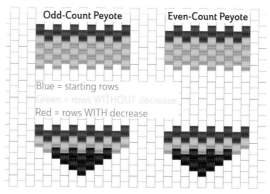

Here, the rows in green have no decrease (same number of beads as the number of beads in the starting rows, in blue) and the rows in red have a decrease (number of beads is fewer than the number of beads in the starting rows, in blue).

Starting a New Row Equal to Set-Up Rows

The following step-by-step instructions will continue to be based on the same diagrams as at the beginning of this tutorial.

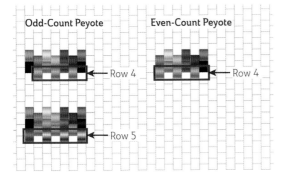

The new row (row 4) is made up of gray beads.

Continuing with Even-Count Peyote

At this stage, the three set-up rows have been completed, and your thread is exiting the green bead going away from the beadwork. To add a new row of gray beads, set off again in the opposite direction.

Pick up the first bead of your new row (gray) and pass your needle through the last bead of the previous row (light brown).

The following beads are stitched on one at a time, passing the needle through the bead from the previous row that is in front of the thread.

Pick up the second bead of your new row (gray) and pass your needle through the bead from the previous row that is in front of the thread (medium brown).

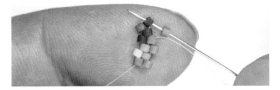

Continue in this manner, one bead at a time, until finished with your row.

Continuing with Odd-Count Peyote

At this stage of the weaving, the three set-up rows are done, and your thread is coming out of the black bead toward the middle of the weaving.

The diagram to the left shows the two new rows to be added: first row 4, comprising three gray beads, and then row 5, which is three gold beads and one turquoise bead.

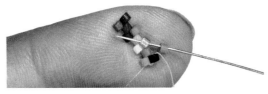

Pick up the first bead of your new row (gray) and pass your needle through the next-to-last bead of the previous row (light brown).

The following beads are stitched on one by one, passing the needle through the bead from the previous row that is in front of the thread.

Pick up the second bead of your new row (gray), and pass your needle through the bead from the previous row that is in front of the thread.

Continue in this manner, one bead at a time, until your row 4 is finished.

With row 4 completed, your thread is exiting the dark brown bead going away from the beadwork. To add the new row of beads, row 5, start back in the opposite direction.

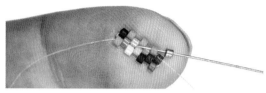

Pick up the first bead of the new row (gold) and pass your needle through the last bead of the previous row (gray).

The following beads are stitched on one at a time, passing the needle through the bead that is in front of the thread.

When all the gold beads are stitched on, here is how to position the last bead (turquoise) of your new row.

First pick up the last bead of row 5 (turquoise) and then pass through the black bead (the last bead of row 3), going back toward the middle of the beadwork.

To attach the last bead of the new row, return toward the middle of the beadwork, passing through the last bead of row 3.

Before you can start the new row, move your thread to the right spot, following the path shown below.

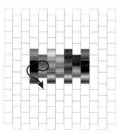

Path to follow to move the thread to the right place to be able to start the next row.

Starting a New Row with a Decrease

For all the cases of a new row with a decrease shown here, the principle is to move the thread to the right spot before being able to add a new row.

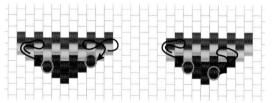

Paths to follow to move the thread to the right place in order to start a new row with a decrease (the circled bead indicates the first bead of the new decrease row).

FINISHING A PROJECT

Once your last bead has been sewn on, finish your project properly following the same method used for the brick stitch (see page 28).

CHANGING THREAD

To change thread in peyote stitch beadwork, follow the same method used for brick stitch (see page 28).

CIRCULAR PEYOTE STITCHES

CIRCULAR PEYOTE

You can quickly make pretty circles with the very easy circular peyote stitch. For this technique, the most important thing is to not apply tension to the thread when stitching so that the beading lies flat. The following step-by-step instructions are based on the beadwork below.

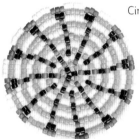

Circular peyote stitch starts in the center, stitching on beads around a small triangle of three beads, increasing in size round by round. In this project, each round was made in a different color (dark blue/orange/blue-gray/white).

Prepare your thread (about 3 ft./1 m long) and your needle. Don't knot the end of the thread.

> **NOTE**
>
> As the work is done in the round, we talk about rounds rather than rows.

Round 1: Set-up round. Pick up the 3 center beads and pass through all of the beads twice again, starting with the first, in order to create a circle with the thread.

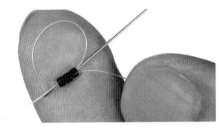

Pull on the thread until the beads form a sort of small triangle.

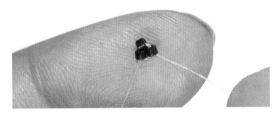

The starting triangle is created. Each new round will be stitched on around it.

Round 2: 2 beads together. The second round is formed by the orange beads. Pick up 2 beads for each stitch. These 2 beads are going to be inserted between beads in the starting round. Pick up 2 orange beads, and then pass through the dark blue bead from the previous round that is in front of the thread.

Repeat this stitch two more times to finish a complete round.

At the end of this round, stitch through (step up through) the first orange bead of the round you just completed.

Your thread is now correctly positioned to begin a new round.

Round 3: Bead by bead. Each bead is inserted between the beads from the previous round. Repeat 6 times to complete the round.

> **NOTE**
>
> Don't forget to stitch through the first bead of the round that was just completed so that you can step up and start the next one in the right place.

Beginning of round 3: the first bead has been added.

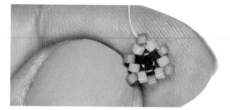

End of round 3: all the beads have been stitched on; the thread is exiting up through the first bead in the row.

Complete all the other rounds following the same principle, each with a specific number of beads per stitch.

Round 4: 2 beads together. Each set of 2 beads is inserted between each bead from the previous round (6 times).

Rounds 5–7: Bead by bead. Each bead is inserted between each bead from the previous round (12 times).

Round 8: 2 beads together. Each set of 2 beads is inserted between each bead from the previous round (12 times). At the end of this round, stitch through the first 2 beads of the round.

Round 9: Bead by bead. Each bead is inserted between each set of 2 beads from the previous round. So, after picking up 1 bead, stitch through the 2 beads from the previous round (12 times).

> **NOTE**
>
> From here on, be sure when you add beads that the beadwork is very supple. Keep your tension loose so that the beadwork remains flat.

Round 10: 3 beads together. Each set of 3 beads is inserted between each bead from the previous round. So, after picking up 3 beads, stitch through the bead from the previous round (12 times). At the end of this round, stitch through the first 3 beads of the round.

Round 11: Bead by bead between each set of 3 beads from the previous round (12 times).

Round 12: 3 beads together between the beads from the previous round (12 times).

Round 13: Bead by bead between each set of 3 beads from the previous round (12 times).

Round 14: 4 beads together between the beads from the previous round (12 times).

Round 15: Bead by bead between each set of 4 beads from the previous round (12 times).

Round 16: 4 beads together between the beads from the previous round (12 times).

Round 17: 2 beads together between each set of 4 beads from the previous round (12 times).

Round 18: 4 beads together between each set of 2 beads from the previous round (12 times).

Round 19: 3 beads together between each set of 4 beads from the previous round (12 times).

Round 20: 4 beads together between each set of 3 beads from the previous round (12 times).

At the end, weave the threads through the beads and cut them.

HEXAGONAL PEYOTE

Here you will find the method used to make hexagons, as well as a second method for making circles. In fact, the first rounds of hexagonal peyote stitch are circular in shape. As the stitching of the shape continues, sides and corners are formed, and more and more clearly you can see the six sides of the hexagon appear.

> ### NOTE
>
> As the work is done in the round, we talk about rounds rather than rows.

The following step-by-step instructions are based on the beadwork below.

The hexagonal peyote stitch starts in the center. The rounds are stitched around a circle of six beads that increases in size as the rounds are added. In this project, each round was made in a different color (dark blue/orange/blue-gray/white).

Prepare your thread (about 3 ft./1 m long) and your needle. Don't knot the end of the thread.

Round 1: Set-up round. Pick up the 6 center beads and pass through all of the beads twice again, starting with the first, in order to create a circle with the thread.

Pull on the thread until the beads form a small circle. Don't pull the beads too tightly together.

The starting circle is created. Each new round will be stitched on around it.

Round 2: Bead by bead. The second round is formed by the orange beads. This round is stitched by picking up 1 bead for each stitch. Each bead is inserted between each of the beads in the starting round. Pick up 1 orange bead, and then stitch through the dark blue bead from the previous round that is in front of the thread.

Repeat this stitch five more times to finish a complete round.

At the end of this round, stitch through the first orange bead of the round you just completed.

Your thread is now correctly positioned to begin a new round.

Round 3: Bead by bead. Each bead is inserted between the beads from the previous round. Repeat 6 times to complete the round.

> **NOTE**
>
> Don't forget to stitch through the first bead of the round that was just completed so that you can step up and start the next one in the right place each time.

Complete all the other rounds following the same principle, each with a specific number of beads per stitch.

Round 4: 2 beads together. Each set of 2 beads is inserted between the beads from the previous round (6 times).

Rounds 5 and 6: Bead by bead (12 times).

Round 7: Alternating 1 bead/2 beads together. Each side is formed of one bead, and each corner comprises 2 beads together. The round starts with 1 single bead (side) and then 2 beads together (corner) (6 times).

Round 8: Bead by bead (18 times). Each side is formed of 2 beads stitched on one after the other, and each corner is made of one bead. *Note:* The round starts at the end of a side—that is, by stitching on the second bead of this side, just before one at the corner.

Round 9: Bead by bead (18 times). Each side is formed of 3 beads stitched on one after the other. There is no bead at the corner; they are bypassed this round. *Note:* The round starts at the end of a side—that is, by stitching on the third bead of this side, just before the first one of the next side.

Round 10: 2 beads together at the corner, and then bead by bead along each side. 2 beads together at each corner (6 times) and bead by bead on each side, between each bead from the previous round (1 side = 3 beads stitched on one after the other). *Note:* The round starts with a corner.

Round 11: Bead by bead (24 times). 1 bead at each corner (6 times) and bead by bead on each side, between the beads from the previous round (1 side = 3 beads stitched on one after the other). *Note:* The round starts with a corner.

Round 12: Bead by bead (24 times). Each side comprises 4 beads stitched on one after the other. There is no bead at the corner; they are bypassed this round. *Note:* The round starts at the beginning of a side.

Starting at round 13, repeat rounds 10 to 12 as many times as needed.

> **NOTE**
>
> Up to round 13, there are fairly open corners to give the shape of a circle. Beyond this round, the shape will become more and more that of a hexagon with more distinct corners and sides.

At the end, weave the threads through the beads and cut them.

┌─ IN SUMMARY ─┐

Hexagonal peyote stitch follows the pattern shown below:

Round 1: 6 beads together

Round 2: Bead by bead (6 times)

Round 3: Bead by bead (6 times)

Round 4: 2 beads together (6 times)

Round 5: Bead by bead (12 times)

Round 6: Bead by bead (12 times)

Round 7: Alternating 1 single bead (side) and 2 beads together (corner) (complete sequence 6 times)

Round 8: Bead by bead (18 times)

Round 9: Bead by bead (18 times)

Round 10: 2 beads together (corner) and 2 beads stitched on one after the other (side) (complete sequence 6 times)

Round 11: Bead by bead (24 times)

Round 12: Bead by bead (24 times)

Starting with round 13, repeat rounds 10 to 12 as many times as needed.

How to Transform a Hexagon into a Six-Point Star

This hexagonal peyote stitch can be used to create stars. See instructions on page 122.

PENTAGONAL PEYOTE

The following step-by-step instructions are based on the beadwork below.

The pentagonal peyote stitch starts in the center. The rounds are stitched around a circle of five beads that increases in size as the rounds are added. In this project, each round was made in a different color (dark blue/orange/blue-gray/white).

Prepare your thread (about 3 ft./1 m long) and your needle. Don't knot the end of the thread.

NOTE

As the work is done in the round, we talk about rounds rather than rows.

Round 1: Set-up round. Pick up the 5 center beads and pass through all of the beads twice again, starting with the first, in order to create a circle with the thread.

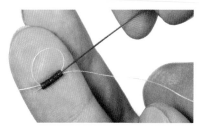

Pull on the thread until the beads form a small circle. Don't pull the beads too tightly together.

The starting circle is created. Each new round will be stitched on around it.

Round 2: Bead by bead. The second round is formed by the orange beads. This round is stitched by picking up 1 bead for each stitch. Each bead is inserted between each of the beads in the starting round. Pick up 1 orange bead, and then stitch through the dark blue bead from the previous round that is in front of the thread.

Repeat this stitch 4 more times to finish a complete round.

At the end of this round, stitch through the first orange bead of the round you just completed.

Your thread is now correctly positioned to begin a new round.

Round 3: 2 beads together. Round 3 is stitched by adding sets of 2 beads. Each set is inserted between the beads from the previous round (5 times).

> **NOTE**
>
> Don't forget to stitch through the first bead of the round that was just completed so that you can step up and start the next one in the right place each time.

Complete all the other rounds following the same principle, each with a specific number of beads per stitch.

Rounds 4 and 5: Bead by bead. Each bead is inserted between the beads from the previous round (10 times).

The thread exits the first bead of the round just completed before going on to the next round.

Round 6: Alternating 1 bead, and then 3 beads together. Each side is formed of one bead, and each corner comprises 3 beads together. Start with 1 single bead (side), and then do 3 beads together (corner) (5 times).

Round 7: Alternating 2 beads together, and then 1 single bead. Each corner is formed of 2 beads together (5 times), and each side comprises one bead between beads from the previous round (1 side = 2 beads stitched on one after the other)

NOTE

To place the set of two beads at each corner, you have to skip over the bead from the previous round, the one in the middle, in order to stitch through the bead that closes the corner.

The round starts at the end of a side. Thus, start by placing one single bead and then two beads together for the corner. Then go back to the sequence (two single beads on the side and two beads together for the corner).

Round 8: Bead by bead. Each bead inserts itself between the beads from the previous round (20 times). Each side is formed of 3 beads stitched on one after the other, and each corner comprises one bead. *Note*: The round starts at the end of a side—that is, by stitching on the third bead of the side, just before the one that forms the corner.

Round 9: Bead by bead. Each bead inserts itself between the beads from the previous round (20 times). Each side is formed of 4 beads stitched on one after the other. There is no bead at the corner; they are bypassed this round. *Note*: The round starts at the end of a side—that is, by stitching on the fourth bead of this side, just before the first one of the next side.

Starting at round 10, repeat rounds 6 to 9 as many times as needed.

At the end, weave the threads through the beads and cut them.

IN SUMMARY

Pentagonal peyote stitch follows the pattern shown below:

Round 1: 5 beads together

Round 2: Bead by bead (5 times)

Round 3: 2 beads together (5 times)

Round 4: Bead by bead (10 times)

Round 5: Bead by bead (10 times)

Round 6: Alternating 1 single bead (side) and 3 beads together (corner) (complete sequence 5 times)

Round 7: 2 beads stitched on one after the other (side) and 2 beads together (corner) (5 times each)

Round 8: Bead by bead (20 times)

Round 9: Bead by bead (20 times)

Starting with round 10, repeat rounds 6 to 9 as many times as needed.

How to Transform a Pentagon into a Five-Point Star

This pentagonal peyote stitch can be used to create stars. See instructions on page 128.

TRIANGULAR PEYOTE

The following step-by-step instructions are based on the beadwork below.

The triangular peyote stitch starts in the center. The rounds are stitched around a circle of three beads that increases in size as the rounds are added. In this project, each round was made in a different color (dark blue/orange/blue-gray/white).

Prepare your thread (about 2–3 ft./50 cm–1 m long; here about 2 ft./50 cm will suffice) and your needle. Don't knot the end of the thread.

> **NOTE**
>
> As the work is done in the round, we talk about rounds rather than rows.

Round 1: Set-up round. Pick up the 3 center beads and pass through all of the beads twice again, starting with the first, in order to create a loop with the thread.

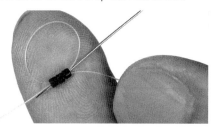

Pull on the thread until the beads form a small triangle. Don't pull the beads too tightly together.

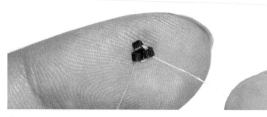

The starting triangle is created. Each new round will be stitched on around it to form the three sides.

Round 2: 2 beads together. The second round is formed by the orange beads. This round is stitched by picking up 2 beads for each stitch. Each set of 2 beads inserts itself between each of the beads in the starting round. Pick up 2 orange beads, and then stitch through the dark blue bead from the previous round that is in front of the thread.

Repeat this stitch two more times to finish a complete round.

At the end of this round, stitch through the first bead of the round you just completed.

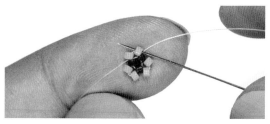

Your thread is now correctly positioned to begin a new round.

The three corners of the triangle are formed. We are now going to start to shape the sides.

Round 3: 2 beads together (corner) and 1 bead (side).

1. Start by picking up 2 beads, and then stitch through the bead facing the one where the thread is exiting.

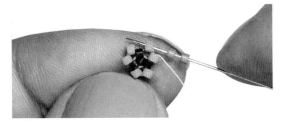

2. Then pick up 1 bead and stitch through the next bead. The first side has just been formed.

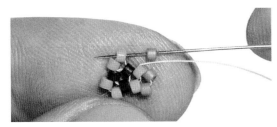

Repeat these two steps two more times to complete the round. Bring the thread up and out through the first bead of the third round to be able to start the next round.

Each new round is stitched following the same principle:

- two beads together at each corner (3);
- bead by bead along the sides—as the beadwork progresses, the sides get wider;

- at the end of the round (3 sides + 3 corners), bring the thread up and out of the first bead from the round just completed (= first bead of first corner).

NOTE

For the last round, stitch only one bead at a time for the entire round (corners and sides).

At the end of your weaving, weave the thread back into the beads and cut it.

IN SUMMARY

Triangular peyote stitch follows the pattern shown below:

Round 1: 3 beads together

Round 2: 2 beads together (3 times)

Round 3: 2 beads together (corner) and 1 bead (side)

Round 4: 2 beads together (corner) and 2 beads stitched consecutively (side) (one bead at a time)

Each new round is stitched following the same principle:

- corner: 2 beads together;
- side: bead by bead (the number of beads increases each round).

The last round is stitched on one bead at a time the entire way around.

EVEN-COUNT AND ODD-COUNT PEYOTE STITCH PATTERNS

∴

Bracelets, cuffs, hair clips, earrings, and necklaces—here are some complete sets of jewelry with variations around a pattern reminiscent of an Art Deco style.

If you feel like creating your own variations, the patterns in this section lend themselves well to experimentation. Show me your versions on Instagram by tagging me in your post @etoiles_pistache.

NOTE

To be sure that you end up with a bracelet that is the right size, use a flexible bracelet that fits well as a guide, and try it on before finishing the beadwork. Don't forget that the width of an end bar, a chain, and a clasp may need to be added to the beadwork to get the total length of the bracelet. In general, the size of the beadwork will be between 5 and 6 in. (13 and 15 cm).

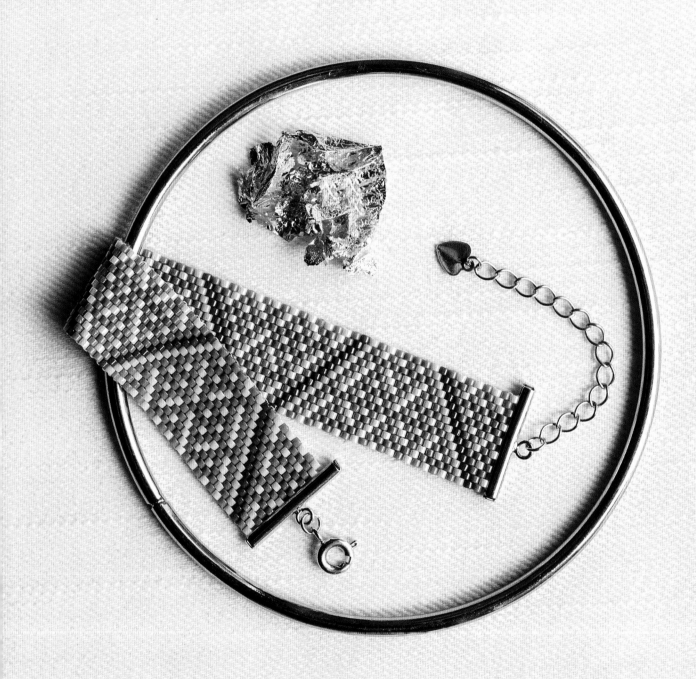

CUFFS AND BRACELETS (WITH END BARS)

**Technique: Odd-Count Peyote Stitch
(see page 86)**

This pattern offers several different widths of
bracelets and cuffs. You can choose between
either blue or orange being dominant and adapt
the length by stopping or repeating the pattern
until the desired size.

WHICH TYPE OF CLASP?

All of these pieces are intended to be attached
to bead weaving end bars or weaving tips (see
page 169). The 13-row charts with pointed ends
are made specifically to fit Perles & Co. bead
weaving tips that are attached to the beads
with the weaving thread.

You can also weave these bracelets to be used
with classic end bars. In this case, start weaving at the beginning of the pattern and repeat
until you reach the desired size.

9- AND 7-ROW BRACELET

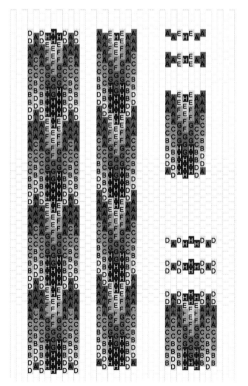

Width: ½ in. (1.2 cm)   Width: ⅜ in. (0.9 cm)

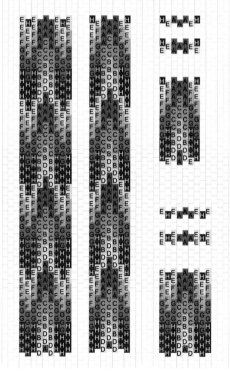

Width: ½ in. (1.2 cm)   Width: ⅜ in. (0.9 cm)

Even-Count and Odd-Count Peyote Stitch Patterns

Color Key

DB-1780	DB-2033	DB-2047	DB-1492
	DB-0760		
DB-1497	DB-0730	DB-1138	DB-0726

A: DB-1780 (Flame Red)
B: DB-2033 (Luminous Creamsicle)
C: DB-2047 (Luminous Bittersweet)
D: DB-1492 (Light Peach)
E: DB-1497 (Light Sky Blue)

F: DB-0760 (Periwinkle) or DB-0730 (Opaque Periwinkle)
G: DB-1138 (Cyan Blue)
H: DB-0726 (Cobalt Blue)

1 Start your piece following the starting rows on the chart you have selected (upper right of chart).

2 Continue stitching the pattern design (on the right side of the chart) until the length is the right size to fit around your wrist.

3 When your piece is the right size, secure and cut your threads. Attach the finishing pieces, chains, and clasps, as well as a little charm for a pretty finish (see detailed instructions on page 169).

TIP

To obtain a piece that is 5 1/8 in./13 cm long, repeat the pattern:

- 4 times for the 7- and 9-row bracelets
- 5 times for the 13-row bracelets
- 5 times for the cuffs (15, 21, and 27 rows)

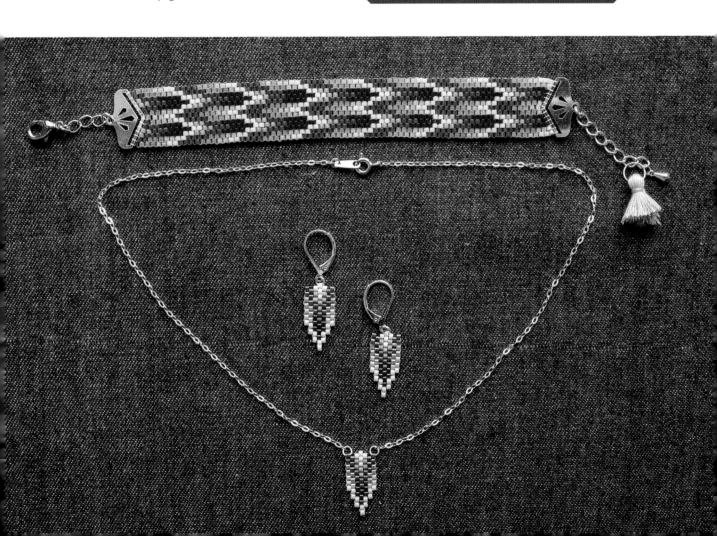

13-ROW BRACELET

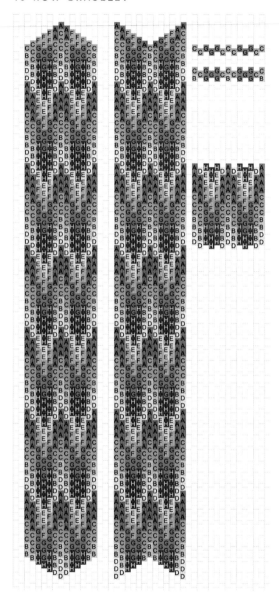

Width: 11/16 in. (1.8 cm)

15-ROW CUFF

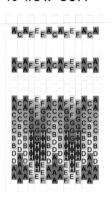

Width: 7/8 in. (2.1 cm)

21-ROW CUFF

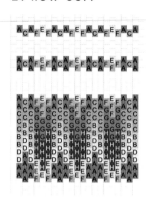

Width: 11/8 in. (2.9 cm)

27-ROW CUFF

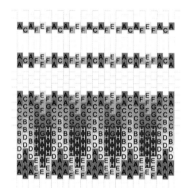

Width: 1/2 in. (3.7 cm)

For Color Key, please refer to the color chart on page 103.

BRACELET (BANGLE OR CHAIN)

Technique: Odd-Count Peyote Stitch (see page 86)

1 Start in the center of the chart, following the starting rows.

2 Work the first part of the pattern and then the second. There are decreases in this piece.

> **NOTE**
>
> Because you start in the center, remember to put your starting beads in the center of the thread. This way you can stitch part 2 without having to add a thread.

3 When your piece is the right size, secure and cut your threads. Attach the beadwork to a plain bangle or a chain (see detailed instructions on pages 168 and 170).

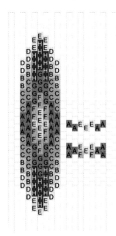

Size of beadwork (without chain): 1⅝ × ⅜ in. (4.2 × 1 cm)

For Color Key, please refer to the color chart on page 103.

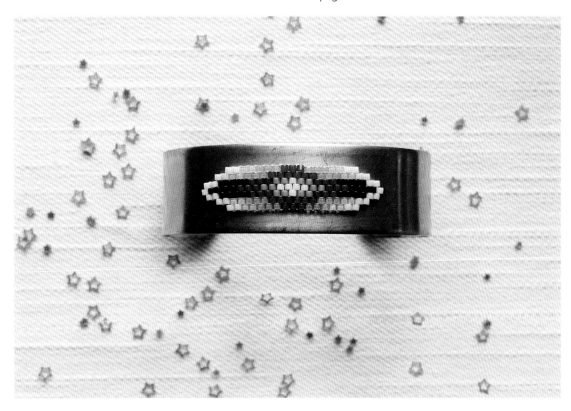

BARRETTE

Technique: Odd-Count Peyote Stitch (see page 86)

With this project, you can create beadwork to personalize a blank barrette back 3⅛ (8 cm) long.

1 Start this piece in the center of the chart, following the starting rows.

> ### NOTE
>
> Because the starting point is in the center, remember to put your first beads in the center of the thread. This way you can stitch part 2 without having to add a thread.

2 Work the first part of the pattern, and then go on to the second part without weaving in the thread. Once both parts are finished, check that the length of the piece matches the length of your barrette back. Add or remove a row on each side if needed.

3 When your piece is the right size, secure and cut your threads. Attach the beadwork to the barrette back (see instructions on page 172).

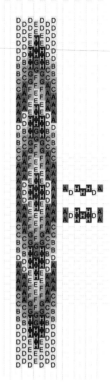

Size: 3⅛ × ⅜ in.
(7.9 × 1 cm)

For Color Key, please refer to the color chart on page 103.

VARIATION

To make a bracelet using this pattern, lengthen by adding rows of light peach (D) beads to each end. To add finishing pieces, follow the method for the bracelet with end bars (see page 169).

NECKLACE AND EARRINGS

Technique: Odd-Count Peyote Stitch (see page 86)

1 Start this piece by following the starting rows in the chart.

2 Follow the direction of the stitching from top to bottom. There are decreases in this piece. You will need to add a bead at the top of the chart, in the center, to finish the beadwork.

3 When you have finished the beadwork, secure and cut your threads. If you are making earrings, make a second one. The next steps depend on what you wish to do with your work.

Option 1: Add a jump ring or bail to the center bead on top (as in the photo of the earrings below).

Option 2: Attach the piece directly to a chain after adding a jump ring at each end (as in the photo of the necklace below).

Size: 7/8 × 3/8 in.
(2.1 × 1 cm)

For Color Key, please refer to the color chart on page 103.

DOTTED BRACELET

Technique: Even-Count Peyote Stitch (see page 86)

This pattern includes various bracelet widths. You can adapt the length of the piece by stopping early or repeating the design until you reach the desired length.

1 Start this piece following the starting rows on the chart selected.

2 Continue stitching per the pattern, repeating the design (on the right side of the chart) until the length is the right size to fit around your wrist.

3 When your piece is the right size, secure and cut your threads. Attach finishing pieces to turn this beadwork into a bracelet (see page 169).

Color Key

DB-0203	DB-2131
DB-2356	DB-2358

A: DB-0203 (Cream Ceylon)
B: DB-2131 (Eucalyptus)
C: DB-2356 (Pale Turquoise)
D: DB-2358 (Evergreen)

TIP

This jewelry is woven in even-count peyote stitch. If you want to create your own variations, this pattern lends itself well to experimentation. Show me your versions on Instagram by tagging me in your post @etoiles_pistache.

10-ROW BRACELET

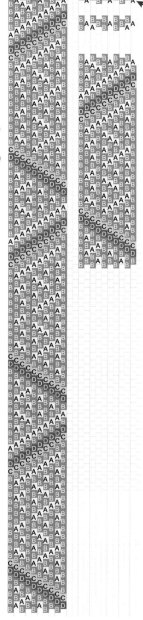

Width: 5/8 in. (1.5 cm)

14-ROW BRACELET

28-ROW BRACELET

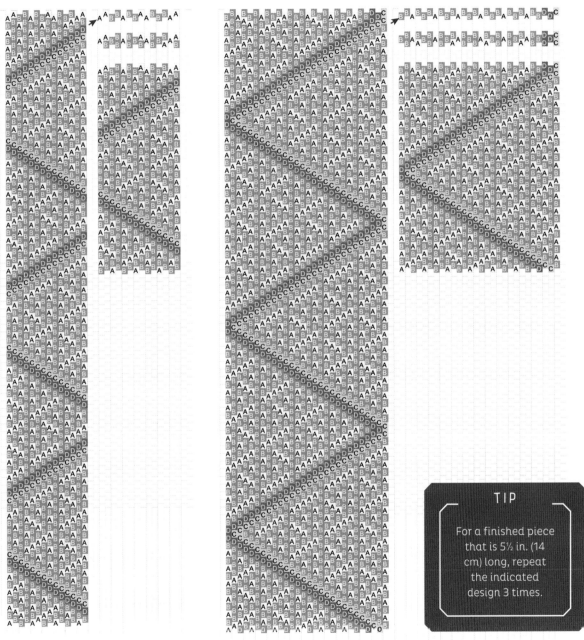

Width: 3/4 in. (2 cm)

Width: 1½ in. (3.8 cm)

> **TIP**
>
> For a finished piece that is 5½ in. (14 cm) long, repeat the indicated design 3 times.

DIAMONDS BRACELET

Technique: Even-Count Peyote Stitch (see page 86)

This pattern includes various widths for bracelets and cuffs. You can adapt the length of the piece by stopping early or repeating the design until you reach the desired size.

BRACELET

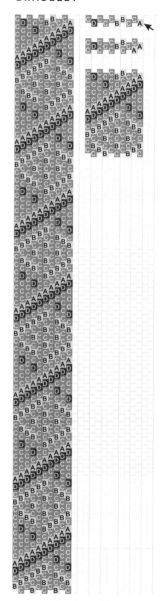

> ## NOTE
>
> The bracelets can also be made using brick stitch.

1 Start this piece following the starting rows on the chart selected. For a chain bracelet without end bars or finishing tips, because the starting point is in the center, remember to put your first beads in the center of the thread. This way you can stitch part 2 without having to add a thread. There are decreases in this piece.

2 For the long bracelet and cuff, continue stitching per the pattern, repeating the design (on the right side of the chart) until the length is the right size to fit your wrist. For the small chain bracelets, follow the chart selected, starting at the point indicated.

3 When your piece is the right size, secure and cut your threads. Attach your desired finishing pieces to complete the bracelet (see page 169).

CHAIN BRACELET WITHOUT END BARS   CHAIN BRACELET WITH END BARS

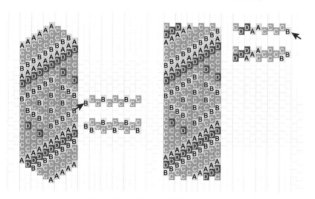

Size: 17/16 × 9/16 in. (3.6 × 1.4 cm)

Color Key

DB-0038   DB-2391   DB-2132   DB-2386

A: DB-0038 (Palladium-Plated)
B: DB-2391 (Oyster)
C: DB-2132 (Bayberry)
D: DB-2386 (Han Blue)

Width: 5/8 in. (1.5 cm)

CUFF

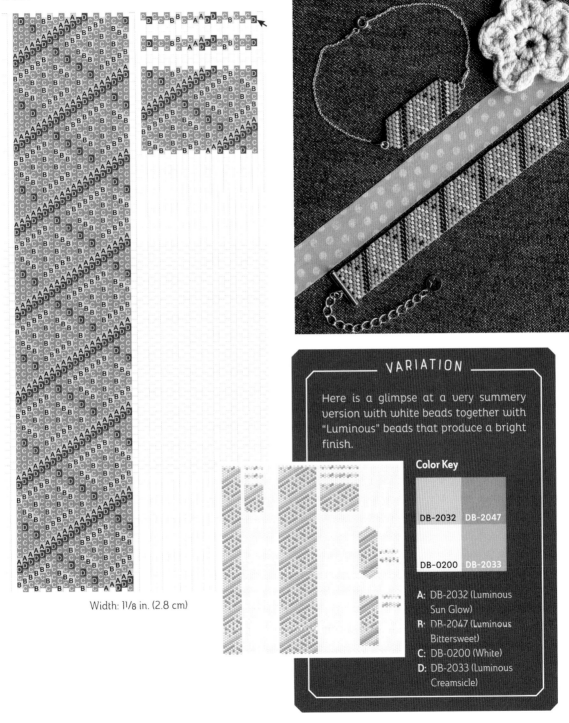

Width: 1⅛ in. (2.8 cm)

VARIATION

Here is a glimpse at a very summery version with white beads together with "Luminous" beads that produce a bright finish.

Color Key

DB-2032	DB-2047
DB-0200	DB-2033

A: DB-2032 (Luminous Sun Glow)
B: DB-2047 (Luminous Bittersweet)
C: DB-0200 (White)
D: DB-2033 (Luminous Creamsicle)

CIRCULAR PEYOTE STITCH PATTERNS

Whether jewelry or decorative pieces, the patterns made with circular peyote stitch can be used in many ways. Here I suggest a few ideas for decorations and jewelry that you can easily modify and adapt.

BRING YOUR BEADWORK TO LIFE

There are several options for the finished use of your projects: jewelry, customized gift wrapping, decorative items, and so forth. To transform your beadwork into accessories, go to page 166.

This beadwork is a variation of Circle 2.

NOTE

The letters used in the instructions refer to the bead colors. At the end of each round, don't forget to "step up" by stitching through the first bead of the round that has just been added.

CIRCLE 1

1 Create this piece following the instructions given below.

Round 1: 3 D beads together

Round 2: 2 B beads together (3 times)

Round 3: C bead by bead (6 times)

Round 4: 2 B beads together (6 times)

Round 5: B bead by bead (12 times)

Rounds 6 and 7: D bead by bead (12 times)

Round 8: 2 A beads together (12 times)

Round 9: A bead by bead between each set of 2 beads from round 8 (12 times)

Round 10: 3 C beads together (12 times)

Round 11: C bead by bead between each set of 3 beads from round 10 (12 times)

Round 12: 3 B beads together (12 times)

Round 13: B bead by bead between each set of 3 beads from round 12 (12 times)

Round 14: 1 E bead + 1 D bead together (12 times)

Round 15: D bead by bead between each set of beads from round 14 (12 times)

2 When your piece is completed, secure and cut your thread (see page 28).

3 There are several ways you can finish up your project. Find all our ideas in part 6, beginning on page 166.

NOTE

If you don't have Bugle beads (E), you can substitute two gold (C) Delica beads.

Size: 13/16 in. (3 cm)

Color Key

DB-0214	DB-2358	DB-2313	DB-0433	DB-0433 BGL1-182

A: DB-0214 (Red Luster)
B: DB-2358 (Evergreen)
C: DB-2313 (Celadon)

D: DB-0433 (Champagne Gold)
E: BGL1-182 (Gold) or a set of 4 DB-0433 (Champagne Gold) beads

CIRCLE 2

1 Create this piece following the instructions given below.

Round 1: 3 D beads together

Round 2: 2 C beads together (3 times)

Round 3: D bead by bead (6 times)

Round 4: 2 A beads together (6 times)

Round 5: D bead by bead (12 times)

Round 6: B bead by bead (12 times)

Round 7: D bead by bead (12 times)

Round 8: E bead by bead (12 times)

Round 9: D bead by bead (12 times)

Round 10: 3 C beads together (12 times)

Round 11: D bead by bead between each set of 3 beads from round 10 (12 times)

Round 12: 3 A beads together (12 times)

Round 13: D bead by bead between each set of 3 beads from round 12 (12 times)

Round 14: F bead by bead (12 times)

Round 15: D bead by bead (12 times)

Round 16: 4 B beads together (12 times)

Round 17: 2 D beads together between each set of 4 beads from round 16 (12 times)

Round 18: 4 C beads together between each set of 2 beads from round 17 (12 times)

Round 19: 3 D beads together between each set of 4 beads from round 18 (12 times)

Round 20: F bead by bead between each set of 3 beads from round 19 (12 times)

Round 21: E bead by bead between each bead or set of beads from round 20 (12 times)

2 When your piece is completed, secure and cut your thread (see page 28).

3 There are several ways you can finish up your project. Find all our ideas in part 6, beginning on page 166.

Size: 1⁵/₈ in. (4.1 cm)

Color Key

DB-0214	DB-2358	DB-2313
DB-1510	BGL1-182	BGL-182

A: DB-0214 (Red Luster)
B: DB-2358 (Evergreen)
C: DB-2313 (Celadon)
D: DB-1510 (Bisque White)
E: BGL1-182 (Gold)
F: BGL-182 (Gold)

NOTE

If you don't have Bugle beads (E and F), you can substitute gold Delica beads: a set of two beads for E and a set of four beads for F.

CIRCLE 3

1 Create this piece following the instructions given below.

Round 1: 3 A beads together

Round 2: 2 A beads together (3 times)

Round 3: B bead by bead (6 times)

Round 4: 2 B beads together (6 times)

Rounds 5 and 6: C bead by bead (12 times)

Round 7: 1 D bead + 1 B bead + 1 D bead together (12 times). Make sure that these 3 beads are positioned to create a small V.

2 When your piece is completed, secure and cut your thread (see page 28).

3 There are several ways you can finish up your project. Find all our ideas in part 6, beginning on page 166.

Color Key

DB-0214	DB-2313	DB-0433	BGL1-182

A: DB-0214 (Red Luster)

B: DB-2313 (Celadon)

C: DB-0433 (Champagne Gold)

D: BGL1-182 (Gold)

NOTE

If you don't have Bugle beads (D), you can substitute a set of two gold Delica beads (C).

Size: 15/16 in. (2.3 cm)

CIRCLE 4

1 Create this piece following the instructions given below.

Round 1: 3 D beads together

Round 2: 2 D beads together (3 times)

Round 3: D bead by bead (6 times)

Round 4: 2 D beads together (6 times)

Round 5: D bead by bead (12 times)

Rounds 6 and 7: A bead by bead (12 times)

Round 8: 2 A beads together (12 times)

Round 9: B bead by bead between each set of 2 beads from round 8 (12 times)

Round 10: 3 B beads together (12 times)

Round 11: B bead by bead between each set of 3 beads from round 10 (12 times)

Round 12: 3 B beads together (12 times)

Round 13: B bead by bead between each set of 3 beads from round 12 (12 times)

Round 14: 4 C beads together (12 times)

Round 15: C bead by bead between each set of 4 beads from round 14 (12 times)

Round 16: 4 C beads together (12 times)

Round 17: 2 C beads together between each set of 4 beads from round 16 (12 times)

Round 18: F bead by bead between each set of 2 beads from round 17 (12 times)

Round 19: 1 E bead between each bead from round 18 (12 times)

Round 20: 3 beads together F + A + F (12 times)

2 When your piece is completed, secure and cut your thread (see page 28).

3 There are several ways you can finish up your project. Find all our ideas in part 6, beginning on page 166.

Size: 2 in. (5 cm)

Color Key

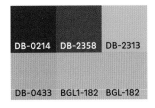

DB-0214 DB-2358 DB-2313

DB-0433 BGL1-182 BGL-182

A: DB-0214 (Red Luster)
B: DB-2358 (Evergreen)
C: DB-2313 (Celadon)
D: DB-0433 (Champagne Gold)
E: BGL1-182 (Gold)
F: BGL-182 (Gold)

NOTE

If you don't have Bugle beads (E and F), you can substitute gold Delica beads (D): a set of two beads for E and a set of four beads for F.

HEXAGONAL PEYOTE STITCH PATTERNS

∙∙∙

Many different shapes can be created using the hexagonal peyote stitch: hexagon, circle (up to a certain diameter), and even stars!

BRING YOUR BEADWORK TO LIFE

There are several options for the finished use of your projects: jewelry, customized gift wrapping, decorative items, and so forth. To transform your beadwork into accessories, go to page 166.

NOTE

The letters used in the instructions refer to the bead colors. At the end of each round, don't forget to "step up" by stitching through the first bead of the round that has just been added.

CIRCLE STAR

Hexagonal peyote stitch can be used to form almost perfect circles up to a certain diameter. Then, as the piece gets bigger, the corners and sides become more and more defined, and the beadwork loses its round shape to form a hexagon.

As this design is fairly small, the corners are still almost invisible, and the shape therefore remains circular.

1 Create this piece following the instructions given below.

Round 1: 6 B beads together

Round 2: B bead by bead (6 times)

Round 3: A bead by bead (6 times)

Round 4: 2 A beads together (6 times)

Round 5: Bead by bead, alternating A, B (6 times)

Round 6: B bead by bead (12 times)

Round 7: 1 B bead by itself (side) and 2 B beads together (corner) (6 times each)

Round 8: Bead by bead, alternating B, A, B (6 times)

Round 9: Bead by bead, alternating A, A, B (6 times)

Round 10: 1 B bead by itself (side) and 2 A beads together (corner) (6 times each)

Round 11: Bead by bead, alternating B, A (12 times)

Round 12: A bead by bead (24 times)

2 When your piece is completed, secure and cut your thread (see page 28).

3 There are several ways you can finish up your project. Find all our ideas in part 6, beginning on page 166.

Color Key

A: DB-0707 (Cobalt)
B: DB-1596 (Agate Blue)

Size: 1 in. (2.5 cm)

Find instructions for the small blue star on page 127.

HEXAGON STAR

1 Create this piece following the instructions given below.

Round 1: 6 A beads together

Rounds 2 and 3: A bead by bead (6 times)

Round 4: 2 A beads together (6 times)

Rounds 5 and 6: A bead by bead (12 times)

Round 7: 1 A bead by itself (side) and 2 A beads together (corner) (6 times each)

Round 8: A bead by bead (18 times)

Round 9: Bead by bead, alternating A, A, B (6 times)

Round 10: 2 A beads together (corner) and 2 B bead stitched consecutively (side) (6 times each)

Round 11: Bead by bead, alternating A, B (12 times)

Round 12: Bead by bead, alternating B, A, A, B (6 times)

Round 13: 3 A beads stitched consecutively (side) and 2 B beads together (corner) (6 times each)

Round 14: 4 A beads stitched consecutively on the sides (6 times) and B at each corner (6 times). The round starts **at the second bead on a side**, stitching A, A, A, B.

Round 15: Bead by bead, alternating A, B, A, A (side) and 1 A bead (corner) (6 times each). The round starts in the **middle of a side, with a B bead**.

Round 16: Bead by bead, alternating A, B, B, A (side) and 2 A beads together (corner) (6 times each). The round starts **at the third bead on a side**, stitching B, A and then corner A + A, subsequently returning to the start of the sequence.

Round 17: Bead by bead, alternating A, B, A, B, A (side) and 1 A bead (corner) (6 times each). The round starts **at the fourth bead on a side**, stitching B, A and then corner A, subsequently returning to the start of the sequence.

Round 18: Bead by bead, alternating A, B, A, A, B, A (on each side, 6 times). The round starts **at the fifth bead on a side**, stitching B, A, and then returning to the start of the sequence.

Size: 1 3/4 × 1 9/16 in. (4.5 × 4 cm)

Color Key

A: DB-0707 (Cobalt)
B: DB-1596 (Agate Blue)

Round 19: Bead by bead, alternating B, A, A, A, B (side) and 2 A beads together (corner) (6 times each). The round starts **at the fifth bead on a side**, stitching B, then corner A + A, and subsequently returning to the start of the sequence.

Round 20: Bead by bead, alternating B, A, A, A, B (6 times) on the sides and A at each corner. The round starts **at the sixth bead on a side**, stitching B, and then corner A, subsequently returning to the start of the sequence.

Round 21: Bead by bead, alternating B, A, A, A, A, A, B (on each side, 6 times). The round starts **at the seventh bead on a side**, stitching B before returning to the start of the sequence.

Round 22: 2 B beads together (corner) and 6 A beads stitched consecutively (side) (6 times each). The round starts **with a corner**.

2 When your piece is completed, secure and cut your thread (see page 28).

3 There are several ways you can finish up your project. Find all our ideas in part 6, beginning on page 166.

6-POINT STAR

1 Create this piece following the instructions given below.

Round 1: 6 A beads together

Rounds 2 and 3: A bead by bead (6 times)

Round 4: 2 B beads (6 times)

Round 5: Bead by bead, alternating A, B (6 times)

Round 6: A bead by bead (12 times)

Round 7: A bead by bead (side) and 2 B beads together (corner) (6 times each)

Round 8: B bead by bead (18 times)

Round 9: Bead by bead, alternating B, B, A (6 times)

Round 10: 2 B beads together (corner) and 2 B beads stitched consecutively (side) (6 times each)

Round 11: Bead by bead, alternating B, B, A, B (6 times)

Round 12: Bead by bead, alternating B, A, A, B (6 times)

Round 13: 2 B beads together (corner) and bead by bead, alternating A, 1 bead not stitched, A (side) (6 times each)

Round 14: Bead by bead, alternating B, A, 2 beads not stitched, A, B (6 times)

Round 15: Bead by bead, alternating A, 3 beads not stitched, A (6 times)

Round 16: 2 A beads together (corner) and 4 beads not stitched (side) (6 times each)

Round 17: 1 A bead by itself (corner) and 5 beads not stitched (side) (6 times each)

2 When your piece is completed, secure and cut your thread (see page 28).

3 There are several ways you can finish up your project. Find all our ideas in part 6, beginning on page 166.

SECTIONS NOT STITCHED

This design includes places where you bypass a part of the stitching sequence to leave an empty space, where the bead(s) would have been stitched, before continuing with the regular sequence of stitching. Pass the thread through the beads forming the edges of the piece (going down toward the center of the design and then back up to the point where the stitching is to be picked up again). With each round, the part of the sequence that is skipped becomes wider.

Color Key

A: DB-0707 (Cobalt)
B: DB-1596 (Agate Blue)

Find instructions for the small 5-point blue star on page 127.

Size: 1¹/₄ × 1¹/₈ in.
(3.3 × 2.9 cm)

PENTAGONAL PEYOTE STITCH PATTERNS

Different sizes of pentagons as well as five-point stars can be created using the pentagonal peyote stitch!

BRING YOUR BEADWORK TO LIFE

There are several options for the finished use of your projects: jewelry, customized gift wrapping, decorative items, and so forth. To transform your beadwork into accessories, go to page 166.

NOTE

The letters used in the instructions refer to the bead colors. At the end of each round, don't forget to "step up" by stitching through the first bead of the round that has just been added.

BLUE PANSY

1 Create this piece following the instructions given below.

Round 1: 5 A beads together.

Round 2: A bead by bead (5 times).

Round 3: 2 A beads together (5 times).

Rounds 4 and 5: A bead by bead (10 times).

Round 6: 1 A bead by itself (side) and 3 beads together A + B + A (corner) (5 times each). The round starts with a side.

Round 7: 2 A beads stitched consecutively (side) and 2 A beads together (corner) (5 times each). The round starts with the **end of a side**. Place 1 A bead followed by the 2 corner beads, and then start at beginning of sequence.

Round 8: 3 A beads stitched consecutively (side) and 1 C bead by itself (corner) (5 times each). The round starts with the **end of a side**. Place 1 A bead, followed by the C corner bead, and then start at beginning of sequence.

Round 9: Bead by bead, alternating B, A, A, B (5 times). The round starts at the **end of a side**. Place 1 B bead, and then start at beginning of sequence.

Round 10: 3 beads together C + D + C (corner) and bead by bead, alternating B, A, B (side) (5 times each). The round starts with a **corner**.

Round 11: 2 D beads together (corner) and bead by bead, alternating C, B, B, C (side) (5 times each). The round starts with a **corner**.

Round 12: 1 D bead by itself (corner) and bead by bead, alternating C, C, B, C, C (side) (5 times each).

Round 13: C bead by bead (30 times). The round starts with a **side**.

Round 14: 5 C beads stitched consecutively (side) and 3 C beads together (corner) (5 times each). The round starts with a **side**.

2 When your piece is completed, secure and cut your thread (see page 28).

3 There are several ways you can finish up your project. Find all our ideas in part 6, beginning on page 166.

Size: 13/16 × 13/16 in. (3 × 3 cm)

Color Key

DB-1785	DB-0277
DB-1527	DB-0040

A: DB-1785 (Cobalt Blue)
B: DB-0277 (Cobalt)
C: DB-1527 (Agate Blue)
D: DB-0040 (Copper)

SMALL 5-POINT STAR

This little star has soft, rounded corners.

1 Create this piece following the instructions given below.

Round 1: 5 D beads together.

Round 2: D bead by bead (5 times).

Round 3: 2 A beads together (5 times).

Rounds 4 and 5: A bead by bead (10 times).

Round 6: 1 D bead by itself (side) and 3 A beads together (corner) (5 times each). The round starts with a **side**.

Round 7: 2 D beads stitched consecutively (side) and 2 A beads together (corner) (5 times each). The round starts with the **end of a side**. Place 1 A bead, followed by the 2 corner beads, and then start the sequence at the beginning.

Round 8: Bead by bead, alternating D, 1 bead not stitched, D (side) and 1 A bead by itself (corner) (5 times each). The round starts with the **end of a side**.

Round 9: D bead by bead. Position the thread to start at the end of a side. Place 1 bead on either side of the corner. Pass the thread through the beads that form the edge and come up at the last D bead. Then stitch the 2 beads on either side of the corner. Repeat these steps until the end of the round.

Round 10: 3 D beads together (corner) and 3 beads not stitched (side) (5 times each).

2 When your piece is completed, secure and cut your thread (see page 28).

3 There are several ways you can finish up your project. Find all our ideas in part 6, beginning on page 166.

SECTIONS NOT STITCHED

This design includes places where you bypass a part of the stitching sequence to leave an empty space, where the bead(s) would have been stitched, before continuing with the regular sequence of stitching. Pass the thread through the beads forming the edges of the piece (going down toward the center of the design and then back up to the point where the stitching is to be picked up again). With each round, the part of the sequence that is skipped becomes wider.

Size: 7/8 × 7/8 in. (2.2 × 2.2 cm)

Color Key

DB-1785	DB-0277
DB-1527	DB-0040

A: DB-1785 (Cobalt Blue)
B: DB-0277 (Cobalt)
C: DB-1527 (Agate Blue)
D: DB-0040 (Copper)

5-POINT STAR

1 Create this piece following the instructions given below.

Round 1: 5 B beads together.

Round 2: B bead by bead (5 times).

Round 3: 2 B beads together (5 times).

Rounds 4 and 5: B bead by bead (10 times).

Round 6: 1 D bead by itself (side) and 3 B beads together (corner) (5 times each). The round starts with a **side**.

Round 7: 2 D beads stitched consecutively (side) and 2 B beads together (corner) (5 times each). The round starts with the **end of a side**. Place 1 D bead, followed by the 2 corner beads, and then start the sequence at the beginning.

Round 8: Bead by bead, alternating D, 1 bead not stitched, D (5 times) and 1 B bead by itself (corner) (5 times). The round starts with the **end of a side**.

Round 9: D bead by bead. Position the thread to start at the end of a side. Place 1 bead on either side of the corner. Pass the thread through the beads that form the edge and come up at the last D bead. Then stitch the 2 beads on either side of the corner. Repeat these steps until the end of the round.

Round 10: 3 beads together D + B + D (corner) and 3 beads not stitched (side) (5 times each).

Round 11: 2 D beads together (corner) and 4 beads not stitched (side) (5 times each).

Round 12: 1 D bead by itself (corner) and 5 beads not stitched (side) (5 times each).

2 When your piece is completed, secure and cut your thread (see page 28).

3 There are several ways you can finish up your project. Find all our ideas in part 6, beginning on page 166.

SECTIONS NOT STITCHED

This design includes places where you bypass a part of the stitching sequence to leave an empty space, where the bead(s) would have been stitched, before continuing with the regular sequence of stitching. Pass the thread through the beads forming the edges of the piece (going down toward the center of the design and then back up to the point where the stitching is to be picked up again). With each round, the part of the sequence that is skipped becomes wider.

Size: 1 × 1 in. (2.5 × 2.5 cm)

Color Key

A: DB-1785 (Cobalt Blue)
B: DB-0277 (Cobalt)
C: DB-1527 (Agate Blue)
D: DB-0040 (Copper)

PENTAGON STAR

1 Create this piece following the instructions given below.

Round 1: 5 B beads together.

Round 2: B bead by bead (5 times).

Round 3: 2 B beads together (5 times).

Rounds 4 and 5: B bead by bead (10 times).

Round 6: 1 A bead by itself (side) and 3 B beads together (corner) (5 times each). The round starts with a **side**.

Round 7: 2 A beads stitched consecutively (side) and 2 B beads together (corner) (5 times each). The round starts with the **end of a side**: place 1 A bead, followed by the 2 corner beads, and then start at beginning of sequence.

Round 8: Bead by bead, alternating A, D, A (side) and 1 B bead by itself (corner) (5 times each). The round starts with the **end of a side**: place 1 A bead, followed by the B corner bead, and then start at beginning of sequence.

Round 9: Bead by bead, alternating A, D, D, A (side) (5 times). The round starts at the **end of a side**: place 1 A bead, and then start at beginning of sequence.

Round 10: 3 beads together A + B + A (corner) and 3 D beads stitched consecutively (side) (5 times each).

Round 11: 2 A beads together (corner) and 4 D beads stitched consecutively (side) (5 times each). The round starts with a **corner**.

Round 12: 1 A bead by itself (corner) and 5 D beads stitched consecutively (side) (5 times each).

2 When your piece is completed, secure and cut your thread (see page 28).

3 There are several ways you can finish up your project. Find all our ideas in part 6, beginning on page 166.

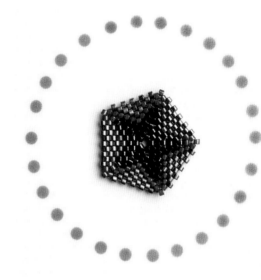

Size: 11/16 × 11/16 in. (2.6 × 2.6 cm)

Color Key

DB-1785	DB-0277
DB-1527	DB-0040

A: DB-1785 (Cobalt Blue)
B: DB-0277 (Cobalt)
C: DB-1527 (Agate Blue)
D: DB-0040 (Copper)

TRIANGULAR PEYOTE STITCH PATTERNS

•:•

Perfect for making some lovely pieces of jewelry, triangles woven in peyote stitch can also find a place in decorative items. Several different-sized triangles would make a very pretty mobile, for example.

BRING YOUR BEADWORK TO LIFE

There are several options for the finished use of your projects: jewelry, customized gift wrapping, decorative items, and so forth. To transform your beadwork into accessories, go to page 166.

NOTE

The letters used in the instructions refer to the bead colors. At the end of each round, don't forget to "step up" by stitching through the first bead of the round that has just been added.

MATCHING SET

The steps below are instructions for making the pendant. If you would like to make the earrings, follow the instructions for the necklace up to round 6. Stitch this last round putting only one bead at each corner (instead of two). Make the second earring in the same way.

1 Create this piece following the instructions given below.

Round 1: 3 beads together A + B + C.

Round 2: 2 beads together C + A, 2 beads together A + B, 2 beads together B + C.

Round 3: 2 beads together C + A (corner 1), 1 A bead by itself (side 1), 2 beads together A + B (corner 2), 1 B bead by itself (side 2), 2 beads together B + C (corner 3), and 1 C bead by itself (side 3).

Round 4: 2 beads together C + A (corner 1), 1 A bead by itself (side 1), 2 beads together A + B (corner 2), 1 B bead by itself (side 2), 2 beads together B + C (corner 3), and 1 C bead by itself (side 3) (2 times each).

Round 5: 2 beads together C + A (corner 1), 1 A bead by itself (side 1), 2 beads together A + B (corner 2), 1 B bead by itself (side 2), 2 beads together B + C (corner 3), and 1 C bead by itself (side 3) (3 times each).

Round 6: 2 D beads together (corner 1), 1 D bead by itself (side 1), 2 D beads together (corner 2), 1 D bead by itself (side 2), 2 D beads together (corner 3), 1 D bead by itself (side 3) (4 times each).

Round 7: 2 beads together A + B (corner 1), 1 B bead by itself (side 1), 2 beads together B + C (corner 2), 1 C bead by itself (side 2), 2 beads together C + A (corner 3), 1 A bead by itself (side 3) (5 times each).

Rounds 8 to 10: Stitch the rounds following the same principle as round 7 (adding 1 additional bead on each side).

Round 11 (last round = corner with only 1 bead): Stitch the entire round with D beads (1 D bead in each corner + 9 D beads stitched consecutively on each side).

2 When your piece is completed, secure and cut your thread (see page 28).

3 If you are making earrings, stitch the design a second time. Assemble into a necklace or earrings (see detailed instructions on page 171 and page 168).

Size: 1¹/₁₆ in. (2.7 cm)   Size: ⁵/₈ in. (1.5 cm)

Color Key

DB-0208	DB-2365
DB-2363	DB-1152

A: DB-0208 (Tan Luster)
B: DB-2365 (Mushroom)
C: DB-2363 (Sesame)
D: DB-1152 (Matte Gold)

POPPIES

Color Key

DB-0200	DB-1708	DB-0745	DB-0068	DB-0010

A: DB-0200 (White)
B: DB-1708 (Ocean Blue)
C: DB-0745 (Matte Transparent Red)
D: DB-0068 (Peach)
E: DB-0010 (Black)

Size: 2 1/8 in. (5.3 cm)

1 Create this piece following the instructions given below.

Round 1: 3 A beads together.

Round 2: 2 A beads together (3 times). Pass the thread up through the first bead of the row.

Round 3: 2 A beads together (corner) and 1 B bead by itself (side) (3 times each).

Round 4: 2 A beads together (corner) and 2 B beads stitched consecutively (side) (3 times each).

Round 5: 2 A beads together (corner) and alternating C, B, C (side) (3 times each).

Round 6: 2 A beads together (corner) and 4 C beads stitched consecutively (side) (3 times each).

Round 7: 2 E beads together (corner) and alternating C, D, B, D, C (side) (3 times each).

Round 8: 2 B beads together (corner) and alternating A, D, C, C, D, A (side) (3 times each).

Round 9: 2 E beads together (corner) and alternating E, C, D, B, D, C, E (side) (3 times each).

Round 10: 2 A beads together (corner) and alternating E, A, C, C, C, C, A, E (side) (3 times each).

Round 11: 2 A beads together (corner) and alternating A, A, A, C, B, C, A, A, A (side) (3 times each).

Round 12: 2 A beads together (corner) and alternating C, A, C, A, B, B, A, C, A, C (side) (3 times each).

Round 13: 2 A beads together (corner) and alternating C, C, C, C, A, B, A, C, C, C, C (side) (3 times each).

Round 14: 2 A beads together (corner) and alternating C, D, A, D, C, A, A, A, C, D, A, D, C (side) (3 times each).

Round 15: 2 A beads together (corner) and alternating B, D, C, C, D, B, A, B, D, C, C, D, B (side) (3 times each).

Round 16: 2 E beads together (corner) and alternating B, C, D, A, D, C, B, B, C, D, A, D, C, B (side) (3 times each).

Round 17: 2 E beads together (corner) and alternating A, B, C, C, C, C, B, A, B, C, C, C, C, B, A (side) (3 times each).

Round 18: 2 E beads together (corner) and alternating A, B, B, C, A, C, B, B, B, C, A, C, B, B, A (side) (3 times each).

Round 19: 2 E beads together (corner) and alternating A, A, B, B, B, B, B, A, B, B, B, B, B, A, A (side) (3 times each).

Round 20: 2 E beads together (corner) and alternating A, B, A, B, B, A, B, B, A, A, B, B, A, B, B, A, B, A (side) (3 times each).

Round 21: 2 A beads together (corner) and alternating A, B, B, A, B, A, B, B, A, B, A, B, B, A, B, A, B, B, A (side) (3 times each).

Round 22 (last round = corner with 1 bead only): 1 A bead by itself (corner) and alternating A, A, B, A, A, A, B, A, A, B, B, A, A, B, A, A, A, B, A, A (side) (3 times each).

2 When your piece is completed, secure and cut your thread (see page 28).

3 This design would be perfect on a long necklace (see detailed instructions on page 171). Add a small tassel to one of the ends for a nice finish.

DIAMOND 1

This pattern is for the earrings in the photo on the right, but you can also use it to make a simple, understated pendant.

1 Create this piece following the instructions given below.

Round 1: 3 A beads together.

Round 2: 2 A beads together (3 times).

Round 3: 2 A beads together (corner) and 1 B bead by itself (3 times each).

Round 4: 2 A beads together (corner) and 2 B beads together (3 times each).

Round 5: 2 A beads together (corner) and 3 beads together A + B + A (3 times each).

Round 6 (last round = corner with only 1 bead):
1 A bead by itself (corner) and 4 A beads together (side) (3 times each).

2 When your piece is completed, secure and cut your thread (see page 28).

3 If you are making earrings, stitch the pattern a second time. Assemble your beadwork into a necklace or earrings (see detailed instructions on pages 171 and 168).

Color Key

| DB-0749 | DB-2033 | DB-0357 |

A: DB-0749 (Gray)
B: DB-2033 (Luminous Creamsicle)
C: DB-0357 (Pale Blue Gray)

Size of earrings: 5/8 in. (1.5 cm)

Size of pendant: 7/8 in. (2.2 cm)

DIAMOND 2

This pattern is for the pendant in the photo on the left, but you can also use it to make earrings.

1 Create this piece following the instructions given below.

Round 1: 3 A beads together.

Round 2: 2 A beads together (3 times).

Round 3: 2 A beads together (corner) and 1 C bead by itself (3 times each).

Round 4: 2 A beads together (corner) and 2 C beads together (3 times each).

Round 5: 2 A beads together (corner) and 3 beads together C + B + C (3 times each).

Round 6: 2 A beads together (corner) and 4 beads together C + B + B + C (3 times each).

Round 7: 2 A beads together (corner) and 5 beads together A + C + B + C + A (3 times each).

Round 8: 2 A beads together (corner) and 6 beads together A + A + C + C + A + A (3 times each).

Round 9 (last round = corner with only 1 bead):
1 A bead by itself (corner) and 7 beads together A + A + A + C + A + A + A (side) (3 times each).

2 When your piece is completed, secure and cut your thread (see page 28).

3 If you are making earrings, stitch the pattern a second time. Assemble your beadwork into a necklace or earrings (see detailed instructions on pages 171 and 168).

PART 3

LOOM WEAVING: METHOD AND PATTERNS

In this section, you will find all the step-by-step instructions on how to weave beads on a bead loom. This technique, which of course requires a loom, produces produces the same result as with the square stitch (see page 146). I recommend this method for medium and large pieces of beadwork (rows of five or more beads), reserving the square stitch technique for smaller beadwork.

NOTE

If you are just starting out, you will find all the information concerning the materials and all the general advice on bead weaving in the introduction section (page 8). This method is distinct from all the others because it requires the use of a loom.

READING A LOOM BEADING CHART

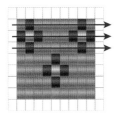

Loom beading is done in a straight line, row by row, always in the same direction.

Each new row of beads is positioned directly above or below the previous one.

The weaving starts at one end of the chart and continues row by row, weaving each bead one after the other.

PREPARING THE LOOM

Loom beading is made up of warp threads set up on the loom and a weft thread formed by the thread that passes through the beads.

In the step-by-step instructions below, we will start with the chart of the smallest rectangle bracelet on page 143.

The first step is to attach the warp threads to the loom. The systems used to attach them differ from one loom to another, but overall the principle remains the same.

Pass the threads over the raised bar, placing them in the individual spaces opposite each other, keeping the same tension, as many times as needed to attach the desired number of warp threads (in this case, seven).

NOTE

Make sure that all the threads have the same tension: it should be neither too loose nor too tight.

Secure your threads by making a slipknot around the peg or by winding tightly around the latter. Cut the thread, leaving about 4 in. (10 cm) of tail after the knot.

Tie your thread to one of the hooks or pegs on the loom. I suggest you make a slipknot, which will be easier to undo than a classic knot.

Attach the number of warp threads needed according to your chart. In this case, a row is six beads wide, so you will need seven warp threads on the loom.

WEAVING

Once your warp threads are ready on the loom, thread your needle (the thread should be about 2½–3 ft./80 cm–1 m). Attach the end of this thread to the outer warp thread with a double knot.

You can position your loom either vertically (facing you) or horizontally. I suggest you try both ways and adopt the one that suits you best.

Tie a double knot on an outer warp thread. This knot is your starting point.

Thread all the beads of the starting row onto your needle; the first one will start from the place where you tied your knot. Here, the first bead is blue.

Take the thread with the beads under the loom's warp threads, bringing the beads underneath.

Place each bead between two threads using your finger to help keep them in place, and then pass your needle through each bead, going over the warp threads.

NOTE

Make sure there is one bead between each warp thread.

After passing your needle through the beads, one or more beads may come loose from the row and fall.

This means that your needle has gone under the warp threads and not over them. In this case, undo the row and start over.

Pull on the thread to snug the beads together. This will bring the warp threads closer together. If the threads resist too much, it means that there is too much tension on your warp threads.

Continue weaving by repeating the same steps.

1. Thread all the beads in the row onto your needle.
2. Take your needle under the warp threads.
3. Place each bead between each warp thread.
4. Slide your needle through all the beads in the row, being sure to pass the needle over the warp threads.

> **TIP**
>
> Once your second row is attached, pass the needle back through the first row and return through the second row so they are solidly in place. Make sure that the two rows are perfectly parallel. Use a flat ruler to push the beads to align the rows if necessary.

FINISHING A PROJECT

The method for finishing off a bead loom weaving project depends on the type of clamp (closure) or backing you will be using. The methods explained in detail on the following page use:

- classic beadwork end bars; or
- a specific backing to which you will glue your piece of beadwork.

If you choose a different type of clamp or closure that requires a different method than the two detailed below, refer to the manufacturer's instructions. In any case, to finish your weaving, first securely attach the last two rows together as you did with the first two: pass the needle through the next-to-last row and then back through the last one. Next, pass the needle back through the next-to-last row and then through the previous ones. Bring the needle out in the middle of a row. Cut your thread.

After bringing the weft thread back through several rows of weaving, cut it in the middle of a row.

Now you can detach your weaving from the loom.

Cut the warp threads as close to the hook or peg as you can so that you have the longest threads possible.

What you do next will depend on the type of finishing method you choose.

Finishing Using a Classic End Bar

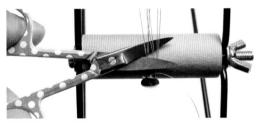

Take the first two warp threads and make a double knot. Repeat as many times as necessary. Cut the threads close to the knots.

Then slide the end bar onto the row of beads. Close the ends of the bar with a small pair of pliers. Now all you have to do is attach a small chain and a clasp. For more on how to attach the end bars, see page 169.

Finishing Using a Backing

If you have chosen to attach your beadwork to a backing (a bangle bracelet or ring blank, for example), here is how you should finish.

This method takes much longer than the previous one, but it results in a finished piece without visible threads.

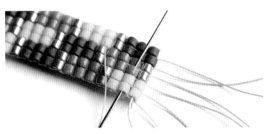

Weave each thread one by one with the needle into the rows of the bracelet, exiting through a middle bead. Cut the thread.

This method should only be used on pieces that are not too wide; avoid using it on cuffs wider than 1 in. (2.5 cm).

CHANGING THREAD

To change the weft thread, go back through the last two rows one more time. Then exit in the middle of a row and cut the thread.

As at the start, make a double knot on the outer warp thread and pick up your weaving where you left off.

LOOM WEAVING PATTERNS

Loom weaving is perfect for making bracelets and cuffs. The patterns that we find very often are Navajo (Native American) styles. Here I am offering some patterns in a different style to bring a little novelty and originality. Each pattern offers variations with widths and/or several color schemes so that you can easily find something to your liking. But here again, feel free to customize the patterns with your own colors!

NOTE

For the length of the bracelets, plan to stop weaving when it measures from 5 to 5½ in. (13 to 14 cm). Adjust the length according to the size of your wrist (± ¼ in. or 1 cm, approximately).

To find the ideal size, remember to take the size of the clamp, the chain, and the closure into account. In my opinion, the ideal size of the woven piece is when it covers the whole upper side of the wrist and down the sides a bit. The other side of the wrist should be dedicated to the clamps and closure system.

TRIANGLE MOTIF BRACELETS

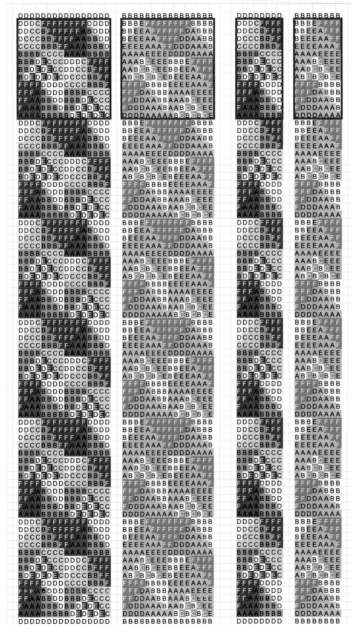

Width: 1 in. (2.4 cm)

Width: ½ in. (1.2 cm)

1 To make these bracelets, go to the tutorial for the loom beading technique starting on page 137. There is no particular difficulty in this loom weaving pattern.

2 Weave the bracelet, repeating the design (in the red square) several times until you have reached the desired length (from 5 to 5½ in./ 13 to 14 cm, approximately).

3 Stop and end your beadwork following the "Finishing Using a Classic End Bar" method; see page 139.

4 For assembly of the bracelet, see the "Bracelet with End Bars" instructions on page 169.

Color Key
(gold, blue, red, pink version)

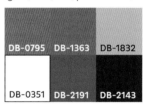

A: DB-0795 (Cinnabar)
B: DB-1363 (Pink Grapefruit)
C: DB-1832 (Gold)
D: DB-0351 (Opaque White)
E: DB-2191 (Silver-Lined Navy)
F: DB-2143 (Navy)
You can use the same shade of blue for E and F if you don't have both of them.

Color Key (pink, khaki, gray version)

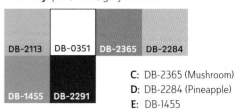

A: DB-2113 (Lychee)
B: DB-0351 (Opaque White)
C: DB-2365 (Mushroom)
D: DB-2284 (Pineapple)
E: DB-1455 (Light Smoke Opal)
F: DB-2291 (Avocado)

RECTANGLE MOTIF BRACELETS

```
CCCCCC        CCCCCCCCCCCC
DDBBCC        DDBBCCDDBBCC
DDAACC        DDAACCDDAACC
DDAACC        DDAACCDDAACC
BBAABB        BBAABBBBAABB
CCBBAA        CCBBAACCBBAA
CCDDAA        CCDDAACCDDAA
CCDDAA        CCDDAACCDDAA
BBDDBB        BBDDBBBBDDBB
AABBDD        AABBDDAABBDD
AACCDD        AACCDDAACCDD
AACCDD        AACCDDAACCDD
BBCCBB        BBCCBBBBCCBB
DDBBCC        DDBBCCDDBBCC
DDAACC        DDAACCDDAACC
DDAACC        DDAACCDDAACC
BBAABB        BBAABBBBAABB
CCBBAA        CCBBAACCBBAA
CCDDAA        CCDDAACCDDAA
CCDDAA        CCDDAACCDDAA
BBDDBB        BBDDBBBBDDBB
AABBDD        AABBDDAABBDD
AACCDD        AACCDDAACCDD
AACCDD        AACCDDAACCDD
BBCCBB        BBCCBBBBCCBB
DDBBCC        DDBBCCDDBBCC
DDAACC        DDAACCDDAACC
DDAACC        DDAACCDDAACC
BBAABB        BBAABBBBAABB
CCBBAA        CCBBAACCBBAA
CCDDAA        CCDDAACCDDAA
CCDDAA        CCDDAACCDDAA
BBDDBB        BBDDBBBBDDBB
AABBDD        AABBDDAABBDD
AACCDD        AACCDDAACCDD
AACCDD        AACCDDAACCDD
BBCCBB        BBCCBBBBCCBB
DDBBCC        DDBBCCDDBBCC
DDAACC        DDAACCDDAACC
DDAACC        DDAACCDDAACC
BBAABB        BBAABBBBAABB
CCBBAA        CCBBAACCBBAA
CCDDAA        CCDDAACCDDAA
CCDDAA        CCDDAACCDDAA
BBDDBB        BBDDBBBBDDBB
AABBDD        AABBDDAABBDD
AACCDD        AACCDDAACCDD
AACCDD        AACCDDAACCDD
BBCCBB        BBCCBBBBCCBB
CCCCCC        CCCCCCCCCCCC
```

Width: 3⁄8 in. Width: 3⁄4 in.
(0.9 cm)   (1.8 cm)

1 To make these bracelets, go to the tutorial for the loom beading technique beginning on page 137. There is no particular difficulty in this loom weaving pattern.

2 Weave the bracelet, repeating the design (in the red square) several times until you have reached the desired length (from 5 to 5½ in./13 to 14 cm, approximately).

3 Stop and end your beadwork following the desired finishing method (end bar or backing).

4 For assembly of the bracelet, see the instructions for the desired finishing method (bracelet with end bars or bangle bracelet).

Color Key

DB-2107	DB-0411	DB-0353	DB-2319

A: DB-2107 (Cedar)
B: DB-0411 (Gold)
C: DB-0353 (Beige)
D: DB-2319 (Navy)

CROSS MOTIF BRACELET

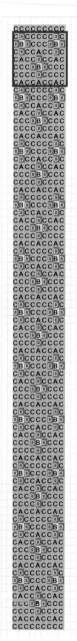

1 To make this bracelet, go to the tutorial for the loom beading technique beginning on page 137. There is no particular difficulty in this loom weaving pattern.

2 Weave the bracelet, repeating the design (in the red square) several times until you have reached the desired length (from 5 to 5½ in./13 to 14 cm, approximately).

3 Stop and end your beadwork following the "Finishing Using a Classic End Bar" method; see page 139.

4 For assembly of the bracelet, see the "Bracelet with End Bars" instructions on page 169.

Color Key

DB-2114	DB-0411	DB-2285	DB-2358

A: DB-2114 (Light Watermelon)
B: DB-0411 (Gold)
C: DB-2285 (Matte Banana)
D: DB-2358 (Evergreen)

Width: ¾ in.
(1.8 cm)

Here, I have chosen to sew the beadwork onto a pouch.
You will find the instructions for the little leaves on page 32.

STRIPED BRACELET

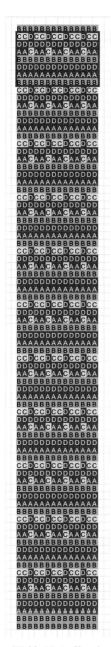

Width: 3/4 in. (2 cm)

1 To make this bracelet, go to the tutorial for the loom beading technique beginning on page 137. There is no particular difficulty in this loom weaving pattern.

2 Weave the bracelet, repeating the design (in the red square) several times until you have reached the desired length (from 5 to 5½ in./13 to 14 cm, approximately).

3 Stop and end your beadwork following the "Finishing Using a Classic End Bar" method; see page 139.

4 For assembly of the bracelet, see the "Bracelet with End Bars" instructions on page 169.

Color Key

DB-1016			
DB-0116	DB-1363	DB-0115	DB-2143

A: DB-1016 (Metallic Rhubarb) or DB-0116 (Wine Luster), for more shine
B: DB-1363 (Pink Grapefruit)
C: DB-0115 (Dark Topaz Gold)
D: DB-2143 (Navy)

PART 4

SQUARE STITCH: METHOD AND PATTERNS

In this section, you will find all the step-by-step instructions on how to stitch beads using the square stitch method. This technique can produce the same result as with bead loom weaving (see page 137) but without a loom. I recommend this method for small pieces of beadwork, reserving loom weaving for larger weaving projects.

NOTE

If you are just starting out, you will find all the information concerning the materials and all the general advice on bead weaving in the introduction section (page 8).

TIP

To improve the life span of the beadwork and simplify the square stitch weaving, I suggest that you use FireLine thread (see details in the "Materials" section, page 9), which is thinner but stiffer than other nylon threads.

READING A BEAD WEAVING CHART

Square stitch is worked in straight lines, woven row by row, in one direction and then the other, stitching on each bead one after the other. Each new row of beads is stacked directly above the previous one. In general, weaving starts at one end of the chart, but you could start at any location.

The first row is worked going bead by bead, from the bottom up. At the end of a row, either the piece is flipped over to again go from the bottom to the top of a row or you could start in the opposite direction, working from top to bottom.

STARTING A PROJECT

As is often the case with bead weaving, the first few rows are the hardest part. After that, the rows come together easily.

In the step-by-step instructions below, we will begin with the following starting diagram.

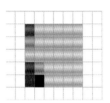

Prepare your thread (about 30 in./80 cm) and your needle. Don't knot the end of the thread.

Pick up all the beads for the first row as seen in the diagram, starting with the one on top. Here, the first bead is brown and the second is green.

Place the beads on the thread so that you have at least 20–24 in. (50–60 cm) of thread between the beads and your needle.

Hold the thread and beads on your finger to keep them in place. Place the beads so that the thread from the beads to the needle is going down and the tail of the thread is going up.

IMPORTANT

At this point, go slowly and carefully, holding your beads firmly between your fingers.

Now pick up the first bead of the second row (here, the black bead). Being careful not to let any loose beads from the first row slip off, pass your needle from top to bottom through the last bead of the first row (the bottom one—the red bead).

Gently pull on your thread without letting the loose beads from the first row fall off. The bottom two beads of the first two rows will move into place, one right next to the other.

Before picking up the second bead, you need to reposition your thread in the bead that has just been placed.

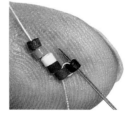

Pass your needle up through the black bead and pull the thread through to the end.

Pick up the second bead of the second row (here, a pink bead) and place it on top of the previous bead.

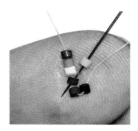

Pass the needle from top to bottom through the blue bead next to it in the first row.

- 147 -

Before picking up the next bead, position your needle in the bead you have just placed.

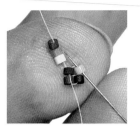

Pass the needle up through the pink bead and gently pull your thread through to the end. The thread must be under the bead that has just been stitched on (the thread tends to slip under the first bead of the row if the thread is pulled too quickly at the end).

Continue in this manner to complete your first two rows.

1. Pick up a bead.

2. Pass the needle from top to bottom through the bead next to it in the first row. The bead will move into place.

3. Pass the needle up through the bead that has just been stitched on so that the thread is in place to continue.

When your row is finished, flip the piece over so that the thread is hanging down. Reinforce the first two rows you just completed by passing the needle back through the first row and then through the second. You can now start your third row.

STARTING A NEW ROW

Two situations can occur when starting a new row:

- The new row starts at the same level as the previous one.

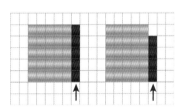

The new row (in red) starts at the same level as the previous row.

- The new row starts one bead set back from the previous row (a decrease).

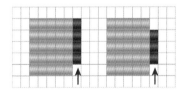

The new row (in green) starts one bead set back compared to the previous row.

There are no increases in square stitch. Check to see which you need to do before starting.

Starting a New Row the Same Width as the Previous Row

To start a new row that begins next to the first bead of the previous row, simply resume working as for the starting row.

Starting a New Row with a Decrease

Here is how to complete the decrease shown in the diagram below.

The new row (in green) begins next to the third bead in the previous row (the red one).

The thread needs to move to where the new row starts. At the moment it is coming out from the bottom.

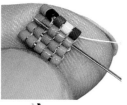

Stitch from the bottom up through the previous row (beige) and exit at the top of the third bead. Pull your thread all the way through.

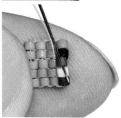

Then stitch from top to bottom through the bead right next to where the new one (the red bead) will go. Pull your thread all the way through.

Your thread is now in the correct place to add the first bead of your new row.

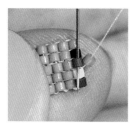

Pick up the first bead of your new row and slide it to the end of the thread so it is snug against the beadwork. Then stitch from top to bottom through the bead next to it.

Before picking up the second bead in the pattern, stitch back through the new bead.

Stitch from bottom to top through the bead just added and gently pull your thread all the way through.

You can now continue stitching bead by bead as usual.

FINISHING A PROJECT

Once your last bead has been sewn on, you must secure the thread by weaving it through several rows (at least four or five so that the thread cannot come loose once you have cut it).

CHANGING THREAD

With square stitch, the ideal would be to avoid changing thread. That is why I suggest this method only for small pieces of beadwork that can be made with 2½ ft. (80 cm) of thread (1 yd./1 m at the most).

Nevertheless, if you must do it, secure your thread as you would when finishing a piece (see above) and cut it. Add the new thread by weaving it through several rows in several directions to secure it. Have the thread exit through the bead where you can pick up where you left off.

MUSTARD JEWELRY SET

For this set of jewelry I started with the mustard color and this deep, lush evergreen that I just could not resist. The cranberry luster and the pink blush balance it all out. I really like this palette, which can be worn in summer as well as winter.

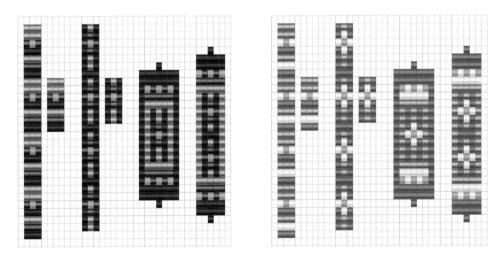

There are an infinite number of ways to change up this set of jewelry with your choice of colors. Here are two more suggestions, or just let your imagination run free! The color references are found on page 157.

RINGS

1 To make these rings, go to the tutorial for the square stitch technique starting on page 147. There are no decreases in these patterns.

2 Make your choice of ring, repeating the design several times. When it is almost long enough to fit around your finger, check the size after each row so that you can stop at the right place.

3 When your ring is the right size, join the two ends, one next to the other, stitching back and forth several times through the first row and then the last row to connect the two ends. Then weave through the following rows to secure the thread before cutting it.

NOTE

To get a ring that fits you, do a test run by joining the two ends of the ring. Simply baste together the end rows, passing your needle once through one row and then through the other. Let the thread hang loosely, and try on your ring.

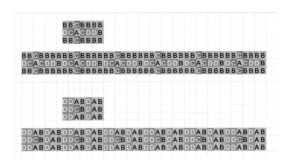

Width: 3/16 in. (0.4 cm)

Color Key

DB-1156	DB-2106	DB-2358	DB-0280

A: DB-1156 (Blush)
B: DB-2106 (Hawthorne)
C: DB-2358 (Evergreen)
D: DB-0280 (Cranberry Luster)

NOTE

The color of the A bead does not hold up well. The blush color will tend to fade on contact with the skin. You can replace it with DB-0191 (Light Copper) or a pink that matches DB-0280 (Cranberry Luster).

BRACELETS

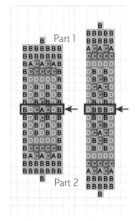

Size: 1 1/4 × 7/16 in. (3.1 × 1.1 cm)

Size: 1 5/8 × 1/4 in. (4.1 × 0.7 cm)

1. To make these bracelets, go to the tutorial for the square stitch technique starting on page 147. There are no decreases in these patterns.

2. Make the starting row (shown in red square) and then work part 1. To add the little bead that will be used to attach the chain and clasp, follow the method for "Starting a New Row with a Decrease" on page 148. Stitch two times through the bead to ensure it is firmly attached. Secure and cut your thread.

3. Work part 2 in the same way, beginning from the opposite side of the starting row. Secure and then cut your thread.

4. To finish off your bracelet, insert a small jump ring in the bead at one of the ends of the piece, slide an end of the chain in the ring, and then close it. Do the same on the other end. If you are using a chain bracelet with a clasp included, your bracelet is finished. If not, all you need to do is attach a clasp at the ends of each length of chain. You will find detailed instructions for the chain bracelet on page 170.

Color Key

DB-1156	DB-2106
DB-2358	DB-0280

A: DB-1156 (Blush)
B: DB-2106 (Hawthorne)
C: DB-2358 (Evergreen)
D: DB-0280 (Cranberry Luster)

The ring on the bottom, glued to a ring blank, is straightened out as shown in the chart on page 156.

TURQUOISE JEWELRY SET

The color turquoise was my starting point for this set of jewelry. Putting it together with a very light khaki or a dark gray anthracite color completely brings out the brightness of the turquoise. I chose to add a touch of light gold, but it could be just as nicely balanced out with silver instead.

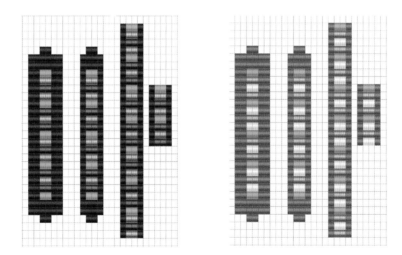

There are an infinite number of ways to change up
this set of jewelry with your choice of colors. You will find
two options here, but feel free to use your own inspiration!

RING

For this ring, I suggest you use Bugle beads, which are shaped like little tubes. They are stitched in the same way as the Delicas.

NOTE

To get a ring that fits you, do a test run by joining the two ends of the ring. Simply baste together the end rows, passing your needle once through one row and then through the other. Let the thread hang loosely, and try on your ring.

1 To make this ring, go to the tutorial for the square stitch technique beginning on page 147. There are no decreases in these patterns.

2 Make the ring, repeating the design several times. When it is almost long enough to fit around your finger, check the size after each row so that you can stop at the right place.

3 When your ring is the right size, join the two ends, one next to the other, stitching back and forth several times through the first row and then the last row in order to connect the two ends. Then weave through the following rows to secure the thread before cutting it.

NOTE

If you don't have Bugle beads, you can substitute two Delica beads.

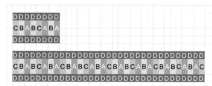

Width: ¼ in. (0.6 cm)

Color Key

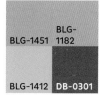

A: BLG-1451 (Gunmetal)
B: BLG-1182 (Gold)
C: BLG-1412 (Turquoise)
D: DB-0301
(Matte Gunmetal)

BRACELETS

For these bracelets, I suggest you use Bugle beads, which are shaped like little tubes. They are stitched in the same way as the Delicas.

1 To make these bracelets, go to the tutorial for the square stitch technique beginning on page 147. There are no decreases in these patterns.

2 Make the starting row (shown in red square) and then work part 1. To add the little bead that will be used to attach the chain and clasp, follow the method for "Starting a New Row with a Decrease" on page 148. Stitch two times through the bead to ensure it is firmly attached. Secure and cut your thread.

3 Work part 2 in the same way, beginning from the opposite side of the starting row. Secure and then cut your thread.

4 To finish off your bracelet, insert a small jump ring in the bead at one of the ends of the beadwork, slide an end of the chain in the ring, and then close it. Do the same on the other end. If you are using a chain bracelet with a clasp included, your bracelet is finished. If not, all you need to do is attach a clasp at the ends of each length of chain. You will find detailed instructions for the chain bracelet on page 170.

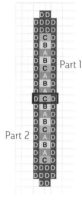

Part 1

Part 2

Size:
1⁹/₁₆ × ¹/₄ in.
(4 × 0.7 cm)

Color Key

BLG-1451   BLG-1182

BLG-1412   DB-0301

A: BLG-1451 (Gunmetal)
B: BLG-1182 (Gold)
C: BLG-1412 (Turquoise)
D: DB-0301 (Matte Gunmetal)

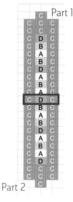

Part 1

Part 2

Size:
1⁹/₁₆ × ³/₈ in.
(4 × 1 cm)

Color Key

BLG-1402   BLG-1182

DB-2282   BLG-1412

A: BLG-1402 (White)
B: BLG-1182 (Gold)
C: DB-2282 (Glazed Smoke)
D: BLG-1412 (Turquoise)

NOTE

If you don't have Bugle beads, you can substitute 2 Delica beads.

PART 5

BEAD EMBROIDERY

I'd like to introduce you to bead embroidery using some traditional embroidery stitches embellished with beads. This technique allows new uses for your brick stitch weaving and opens the doors to a new creative hobby. The numbers you will see in the stitch titles and instructions correspond to the stitches shown in the photo on the next page.

NOTE

If the fabric to be embroidered is thin and loose, it will be necessary to prepare it beforehand using a stabilizer.

MATERIALS

- Embroidery fabric (piece of heavy cotton or linen, Aida cloth) or a fabric item or a piece of clothing
- 1 embroidery hoop
- Embroidery thread
- 11/0 Delica beads, 3 mm or 6 mm Bugle beads, or small round beads
- 1 extra fine needle with narrow eye
- 1 embroidery marking pen
- 1 small pair of scissors

TIP

I really like using the metallic braid from Au Ver à Soie. It is very suitable for bead embroidery and produces a beautiful finished look. If you are embroidering with stranded cotton, I suggest you use two strands.

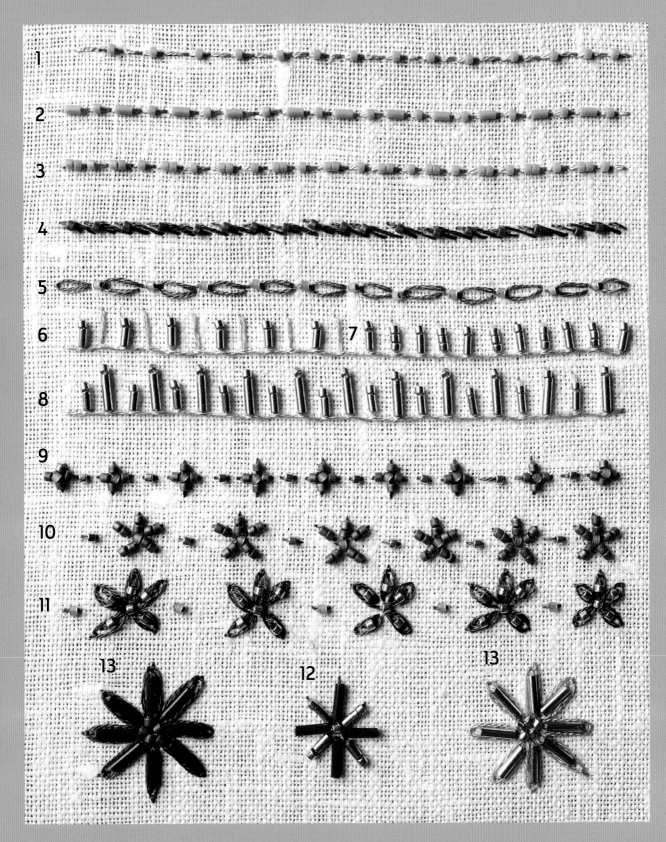

SOME STITCHES TO GET YOU STARTED

Back Stitch (1 to 3)

This is the ideal stitch for embroidering straight or curved lines. It is worked from right to left. The beads can be placed in different ways:

- 1 Delica bead every other stitch (1)
- alternating between 1 Delica 11/0 bead and 1 Bugle 3 mm bead (2)
- alternating between 2 Delica 11/0 beads embroidered together and 1 Delica 11/0 bead (3)

Stem Stitch (4)

Like the back stitch, this stitch is also used to draw lines. It is embroidered from left to right. Place one bead every other stitch. You can also thread on one or two beads with every stitch. In this case, you will have to accentuate the slope of the stitch.

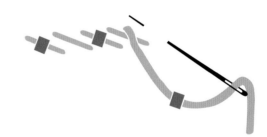

Lazy Daisy Stitch (5)

As its name indicates, this stitch looks like a flower petal. It can be used in a line (chain stitch), but it can also be used to make petals when embroidering flowers or leaves along stems. The beads can then be placed at the end of a petal (5) or in the center of the petals (flower/star 11 and 13).

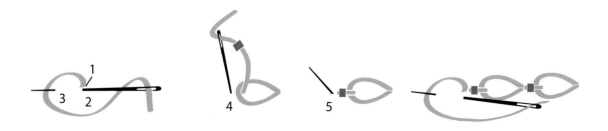

Blanket Stitch (6 to 8)

If you already embroider, you undoubtedly are familiar with the blanket (or buttonhole) stitch. The stitches can be spaced out or placed closer together.

The beads can be placed in every stitch or every other stitch. The height of the stitches can also be varied, changing the number or size of the beads used:

- 1 Bugle 3 mm bead and 1 Delica 11/0 bead embroidered together every other stitch (6)

- alternating between 1 Bugle 3 mm bead and 1 Delica bead embroidered together and 3 Delica 11/0 beads (7)

- alternating between 1 Bugle 3 mm bead and 1 Delica bead embroidered together and 1 Bugle 6 mm bead and 1 Delica bead embroidered together (8)

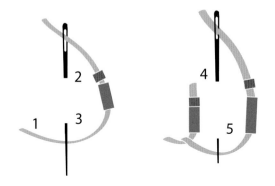

Cross Stitch (9)

This very well-known embroidery stitch can be used to make pretty little flowers when you add beads. In particular, it can be used for making pretty borders. In this case, you can alternate a cross stitch with a small isolated bead.

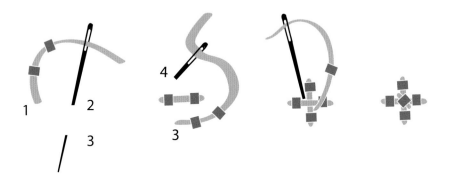

Flowers and Stars (10 to 13)

Bead embroidery can be used to make pretty flowers or stars. By varying the type of stitches, the number of petals (or points, if it is a star), and the size of the beads, you can create quite an assortment of different designs.

NOTE

Design 13, illustrated on page 159, is embroidered following the same principle as Design 12; simply add a few small beads in the center.

DESIGN 10

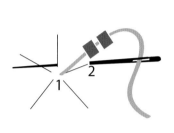   

DESIGN 11

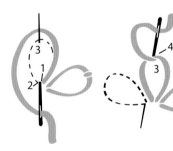   

DESIGN 12

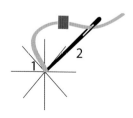 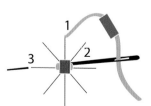 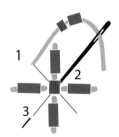 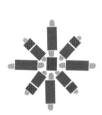

LUCKY EYE

Materials:
- Basic kit (see page 158)
- Hand Beaded Lucky Eye 1 (see page 55)
- Metallic Gold Braid for Embroidery (Au Ver à Soie)

Miyuki Beads:
- Gold Delicas (DB-1832)
- 3 mm and 6 mm Gold Bugles

VARIATION

Feel free to add a few embroidered stars around the beadwork.

1 After making the Lucky Eye 1, place it on the embroidery fabric and trace the upper edge with the marker. Place the fabric in your hoop.

2 Embroider along the traced line in blanket stitch (see page 161), alternating 1 3-mm Bugle bead and 1 Delica bead embroidered together with 1 6-mm Bugle bead and 1 Delica bead embroidered together.

3 After removing the marker line with water or by ironing, glue or sew on the beaded eye.

FORGET-ME-NOTS

Materials:
- Basic kit (see page 158)
- Hand Beaded Forget-Me-Not Bouquet (see page 73)
- Metallic Gold Braid for Embroidery (Au Ver à Soie)

Miyuki Beads:
- Straw Yellow Delicas (DB-2186)

VARIATION

Embroider a few leaves along the stems using the lazy daisy stitch.

1 After making the Forget-Me-Not Bouquet, place the beadwork on the embroidery fabric and draw stems with the marker. Place the fabric in your hoop.

2 Embroider one stem in back stitch, the second in lazy daisy stitch, and the last in stem stitch (see page 160 for all three stitches).

3 After removing the marker line with water or by ironing, glue or sew on the beadwork.

PAIR OF FLOWERED BIRDS

Materials:
- Basic kit (see page 158)
- Flowered Birds in Mirror Image beadwork (see below)
- Metallic Gold Braid for Embroidery (Au Ver à Soie)

Miyuki Beads:
- Jazzberry Delicas (DB-2050)
- Eucalyptus Delicas (DB-2131)
- Navy Delicas (DB-2143)

Size: 1⅛ × 1 9⁄16 in. (2.9 × 4 cm)

Color Key

DB-0631	DB-0868	DB-0674
DB-0352	DB-2041	DB-2131
DB-2143	DB-1807	DB-2050

A: DB-0631 (Gray)
B: DB-0868 (Pink Mist)
C: DB-0674 (Light Topaz)
D: DB-0352 (Cream)
E: DB-2041 (Luminous Honeycomb)
F: DB-2131 (Eucalyptus)
G: DB-2143 (Navy)
H: DB-1807 (Rose Silk Satin)
I: DB-2050 (Jazzberry)

1. After making the Flowered Birds in Mirror Image, place the beadwork on the embroidery fabric and draw a circle around it with the marker, using a small glass as a guide. Place the fabric in your hoop.

2. Embroider along the line with small cross stitch flowers (see page 161), alternating them with a small isolated bead.

3. After removing the marker line with water or by ironing, glue or sew on the beadwork.

This can be used as a decorative piece by framing it in a small embroidery hoop.

 VARIATION

Draw a heart instead of a circle, and embroider several isolated flowers around the beadwork.

PART 6

WHAT TO DO WITH YOUR BEADWORK

In this section, you will find around 20 ideas for things to do with your beadwork, with step-by-step instructions, to find the best use for your creations. Jewelry, decorative items, accessories, and other objects are waiting for you in these pages..

NOTE

As beadwork is relatively supple, I suggest that you stiffen it for some projects, depending on the final use (see page 10).

PIN

The majority of brick stitch beadwork (pages 12 to 83) could be worn as a pin. Used alone or in combination with others, a pin can be worn on any top as well as on a coat.

Materials:
- 1 pin back to match the size of the beadwork
- 1 tube of jewelry glue
- Décopatch varnish and a suitable brush to stiffen the beadwork (optional)
- 1 piece of imitation leather (optional)

1 Stiffen the beadwork to help your pin hold up well; see page 10.

2 If you are not using imitation leather, affix the pin backing to the beadwork with the jewelry glue and your pin is finished. For a more polished finish, place the beadwork on the reverse side of the imitation leather; using a fine marker, trace around the edge as close to the beadwork as possible.

3 Cut out the shape from the imitation leather, following the inside edge of the line. Be sure it does not stick out from the beadwork once glued on.

4 Check that the shape matches that of the beadwork without going over. Cut again if needed before gluing to the beadwork. Let dry, placing it under a book or a fairly heavy object (but not too heavy!).

NOTE

Miyuki beads are glass beads and do not stand up to strong pressure, so be sure that the item you put on top of the beadwork is not too heavy.

5 Finally, glue your pin back to the imitation leather.

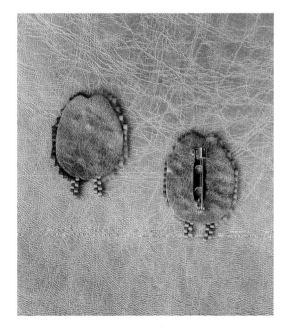

EARRINGS

Some beadwork in this book can be worn as earrings.

Materials:
- 2 earring hooks or lever-back earwires
- 2 jump rings (3 mm or 5 mm × 0.6 mm)
- 2 pairs of flat nose jewelry pliers

1 Stiffen the beadwork; see instructions on page 10.

2 Open one of the rings with the pliers, spreading apart the ends from front to back as seen in the photo, so that you do not distort the shape of the ring and thus weaken it.

3 Slide the ring into the bead and attach one of the lever-back earwires before closing the ring again.

4 Repeat the operation for the second lever-back earring.

BANGLE BRACELET

Rectangular-shaped beadwork, particularly pieces done in peyote stitch or on a loom, can be attached to bangle bracelets. In this case, it is a very quick and simple project.

Materials:
- 1 bangle bracelet matching the width of the beadwork
- Jewelry glue

1 Glue your beadwork to the bracelet.

2 Your bracelet is finished.

I have added end bars (see explanation on next page) to the beadwork in order to be able to attach little tassels, but I could have glued the beadwork directly onto the bangle.

BRACELET WITH END BARS

Several weaving stitches found in this book can be turned into bracelets, particularly peyote stitch, square stitch, and loom weaving.

Materials:
- 2 beadwork end bars matching the width of the beadwork
- 2 jump rings (3 mm or 5 mm × 0.6 mm)
- 1 short length of large, round link chain (or extension chain with clasp or a few jump rings 4–6 mm)
- 1 clasp
- 2 pairs of flat nose jewelry pliers
- 1 small charm (optional)

1 First attach the end bars to the ends of the beadwork. For peyote stitch pieces with ends that are not perfectly straight, 1 bead must be added in front of each bead in the last row. To do this, proceed as if you wanted to make an end of row increase (brick stitch method; see page 25).

2 Open one of the jump rings with the pliers, spreading apart the ends from front to back as seen in the photo on page 168.

3 Slide the ring in the end bar and attach a small chain (or an extension chain). You could also put a few jump rings together to make a small chain yourself.

4 Open another jump ring with the pliers, slide it through the other end bar, and attach the clasp.

5 For a nice finished look, you could add a small charm at the end of the chain.

Special "Perles & Co." Weaving Tips

For 13-row bracelets in the Art Deco jewelry set (page 100), I used Miyuki bead weaving tips created by Perles & Co. These tips are attached directly to the beads with the weaving thread. All instructions are available on their website at https://www.perles andco.co.uk/tutorials/t7221-miyuki-peyote-wo ven-13-row-weaving-bracelet.html.

CHAIN BRACELET

Some small designs can be used to make chain bracelets.

Materials:
- 4 jump rings (3 mm or 5 mm × 0.6 mm)
- 2 lengths of chain to fit your wrist
- 1 clasp
- 1 clasp fastener
- 2 pairs of flat nose jewelry pliers
- 1 small charm (optional)

> **NOTE**
>
> You can insert small beaded designs in chain bracelets, which are practical because they come already assembled with clasps. Be sure that the chain rings can fit into the beads; otherwise they will need to be removed and replaced by two rings of the right thickness.

1. Open one of the rings with the pliers, spreading apart the ends from front to back as seen in the photo on page 168.

2. Slide the ring in the bead, and attach one of the ends of the chain to it before closing it up.

3. Repeat these two steps to attach the other length of chain.

4. If you are using a chain bracelet with a clasp included, your bracelet is finished. If not, attach the clasp and the clasp fastener using the jewelry pliers.

5. For a nice finished look, you could add a small charm at the end of the chain.

RING GLUED TO A RING BLANK

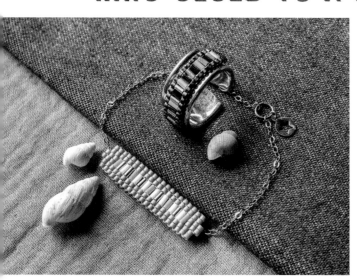

Patterns for woven bead rings are found in the Square Stitch section.

Materials:
- 1 ring blank to fit the beadwork
- Jewelry glue

1. Glue your beadwork to the ring.

2. Your ring is finished.

SHORT OR LONG NECKLACE

Some of the beadwork in this book can be used to make necklaces of varying lengths. Here are a couple of ways to do that.

Materials:
- 4 jump rings (3 mm or 5 mm × 0.6 mm)
- 2 lengths of chain
- 1 clasp
- 1 clasp fastener
- 2 pairs of flat nose jewelry pliers

> ### NOTE
>
> You can use very convenient, already assembled chain necklaces for inserts. Be sure that the chain rings can fit into the beads; otherwise they will need to be removed and replaced by two rings with the right thickness.

1. Open one of the rings with the pliers, spreading apart the ends from front to back as seen in the photo on page 168.

2. Slide the ring in the bead and attach one of the ends of the chain to it before closing it up.

3. Repeat these two steps to attach the other length of chain.

4. Attach the clasp and the clasp fastener to each of the lengths of chain with the jewelry pliers and the two remaining jump rings.

PENDANT

Some of the beadwork in this book can be used to make a pendant to slide onto your choice of chain.

Materials:
- 1 jump ring (3 mm or 5 mm × 0.6 mm)
- 1 pendant bail (or pendant holder)
- 2 pairs of flat nose jewelry pliers

Complete step 1 for the necklace on the previous page. Then slide the ring into the bead and attach the bail before closing it.

BARRETTE, HAIR CLIP, OR HAIR COMB

Rectangular-shaped beadwork (particularly that done in peyote stitch or on a loom) and small brick stitch pieces can make pretty hair accessories.

Materials:
- 1 barrette back (8 cm), or 1 hair clip or 1 hair comb
- Jewelry glue

For the barrette, proceed exactly as for pin mounting on page 167.

> ## NOTE
>
> The chart on page 106 is a perfect fit for an 8 cm barrette. For the hair clip or comb, choose a small design, such as the Spring Flower on page 80 or the Small Leaf on page 65.

For the hair clip or comb, glue the selected beadwork to the backing using the jewelry glue.

POUCH, BAG, PENCIL OR EYEGLASSES CASE

Most of the beadwork in this book can be used to customize any accessory. If you are a sewist, even a beginner (like me!), you can make your own pouch, bag, or case, and sew your beadwork onto it. You can also add bead embroidery to any of them.

Materials:
- 1 fabric item you wish to personalize
- 1 beading needle
- Sewing or beading thread
- Jewelry glue

Glue the design(s) onto the fabric. To attach it even better, sew a few stitches around the edge of the beadwork. To do this, stitch around a thread bridge joining two beads together or pass the needle through the inside of a bead before stitching into the fabric. Add some bead embroidery if you wish; see the stitches starting on page 160.

PERSONALIZED NOTEBOOK

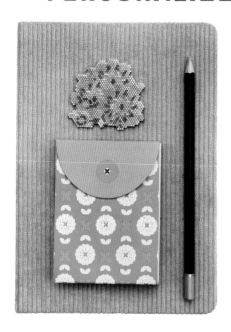

The majority of brick stitch beadwork can be glued to the cover of a notebook. This is a very simple and quick way to personalize your notebooks; they will stand out and be easily recognizable.

Materials:
- 1 notebook with a cover that can be glued
- Jewelry glue

1 Glue your beadwork to the cover of the notebook.

2 Your notebook is finished.

KEYCHAIN

Most of the beadwork in this book can be used to make a pretty keychain.

Materials:
- 1 key ring with chain
- 1 jump ring (3 mm or 5 mm × 0.6 mm)
- 2 pairs of flat nose jewelry pliers

1 Open one of the rings with the pliers, spreading apart the ends from front to back as seen in the photo on page 168.

2 Slide the bead onto the ring and attach the keychain to the jump ring before closing it.

BOOKMARK

A bookmark will make an original gift or will follow along with you wherever you read.

Materials:
- 1 bookmark base
- 1 jump ring
- 2 pairs of flat nose jewelry pliers

There are bookmark bases to which you can affix the beadwork. To do this, put a jump ring through a bead in the piece of beadwork, and then attach the bookmark to this ring.

You can also cut a rectangular bookmark out of cardstock and place an eyelet in it. After placing an open jump ring in one of the beads in the beadwork, you can slide a small cord through it and attach it to the bookmark.